Student Success

How to do better in college and still have time for your friends

SECOND EDITION

TIM WALTER
Rhode Island College

AL SIEBERT
Oregon School of Education

HOLT, RINEHART AND WINSTON
New York   Chicago   San Francisco   Philadelphia
Montreal   Toronto   London   Sydney   Tokyo
Mexico City   Rio de Janeiro   Madrid

Library of Congress Cataloging in Publication Data

Walter, Tim.
  Student success.

  1. Study, Method of. 2. Success. I. Siebert, Al,
joint author. II. Title.
LB1049.W27   1981   378'.1702812   80-27719

ISBN 0-03-058184-2

Address correspondence to: 383 Madison Avenue
                           New York, N.Y. 10017

CBS College Publishing
Holt, Rinehart and Winston
The Dryden Press
Saunders College Publishing

About this book

Student Success brings together the best information available on doing well in college. It covers major factors that help or hinder students at all levels—from undergraduates to graduates.

–*Specific study skills*: the best ways to take notes, study for tests, write papers, and pass tests.

–*Time management*: how to develop a study schedule that keeps you from studying too much, provides enough study time for you to accomplish your study goals, and reserves ample time for athletics, music, social life, working, important causes, or other interests.

–*Habits and attitudes*: how to acquire habits and attitudes that lead to success in college and success in life.

–*Working with instructors*: getting the most out of every course by working with instructors rather than being misled by common myths about instructors.

–*Teaching styles and learning styles*: what to do when you don't have a good match between your learning style and an instructor's teaching style.

–*Building good friendships*: lack of friends is a major distraction for some students. *Student Success* devotes a chapter to friendships.

–*Self-actualization*: how to use college experiences as a starting point for life-long self-development.

–*Using all the support services on campus*: how to take advantage of everything your college has to offer.

Discovering Your Third Choice

Many students seem to believe they have only two choices in college. One choice is to become a bookworm, with very little time allowed for recreation, social activities, or outside interests.

The other choice is not to allow school to interfere with more important interests. For such students, studying is an interruption and done when necessary to maintain the required "C" level.

Some students know that they have a third choice. They study effectively and still have time for other major involvements. Not many students can exercise their third choice. That is why we wrote *Student Success.* We want to show you that you can get a good education and still have time for friends, athletics, recreation, music, and other activities.

iii

Student Success shows you how to be a complete person. Anyone can be one-sided. Anyone can get good grades by being a bookworm. Anyone can totally focus on campus activities or social causes and rarely study. But the person who has learned to study smarter can get a solid education while working, playing, and enjoying life. The choice is yours!

About the authors

Tim Walter and Al Siebert are co-authors of the Student Manual that accompanies *Understanding Human Behavior* by James V. McConnell. They both earned Ph.D.'s in psychology from the University of Michigan.

Tim is now with the Psychology Department at Rhode Island College. His background is in behavioral and educational psychology. He has years of experience teaching learning and reading skills courses. Over the past decade he has developed a psychology course, "The Successful Student," taken by hundreds of students.

Al teaches part time at Portland State University in Oregon. He specializes in applying the principles of personality development in teaching methods and developed the concept "The Survivor Personality."

By working together, Tim and Al combine behavioral techniques with humanistic principles. In *Student Success* they integrate the full range of what psychologists know about "learning how to learn." The result is a practical, effective book.

How to use this book

First, take a minute to skim through this book. Ask yourself questions about it. Do that now.

If you usually ask questions as you skim material, that is great! You have an active mind and quickly grasp the main ideas in written material. If you glanced through the book without asking questions, that is a clue for improvement. Learning to ask questions is one of the first habits that you may want to work on.

Here are some questions that might be asked while skimming through the book:

What must I do to be successful?
How can studying be easier?
Can I improve my intelligence?
What are some tips on how to pass exams better?
How can I write better papers more rapidly without making them longer?
Why Is there a whole chapter on study goals?
× What do successful students do?
How can I enjoy courses taught by instructors I dislike?
× How can I have more good friends?
What does it mean to view life as a school?
× Who can help me when I need help to succeed?

Second, don't think you have to do everything all at once! Pick several skill areas that you believe are most likely to be quickly helpful and try them first. Skip sections that you don't want to use yet.

This book is a compilation of many practical tips and psychological principles. It can take a long time to learn how to use them all. The key to the successful use of the book is not to try to do it all, at least not at the start. You'll burn yourself out. Try a few things until they become habits, and then work on building a few more habits. This is a book you will want to keep and review every few months.

Remember that habits take time to acquire. Habits take months to develop but once you have them, you have them for life!

CONTENTS

CHAPTER 4
DOING WELL ON TESTS 39

CHAPTER 5
WRITING EFFECTIVE PAPERS: USING YOUR LIBRARY
WELL 49

CHAPTER 6
SETTING AND ACHIEVING YOUR STUDY GOALS 59

CHAPTER 7
ERRONEOUS BELIEFS ABOUT INSTRUCTORS
AND MATCHING LEARNING AND TEACHING STYLES 72

CHAPTER 1

Taking Responsibility for your education

BE RESPONSIBLE FOR YOURSELF

How much do you feel responsible for the way your life goes? Do you take credit for your successes? For your failures?

Successful students feel responsible for themselves. People having trouble in college tend to dismiss success as "good luck" and blame others for their woes. Perhaps you've heard students say

"I sure was lucky to get a 'B' in Math."

"I could get to class on time if it weren't for _____ !"

"She gave me an 'A' on my paper. I really lucked out."

"How can you enjoy going to a class taught by a guy who _____ ?"

"Nobody at this college cares about students. There's no way we can do well here."

Such statements are made by people who don't feel responsible for what happens in their lives. They don't see the relationship between what they do and the results they get.

To do better in college make your success or failure your responsibility. Say to yourself, "My success is my responsibility. It is not dependent upon instructors, employers, relatives, friends, classmates, administrators, rules, regulations, or fate. I get credit for my successes! I am responsible for my successes and failures."

As an indicator of how much you are now a person with a strong sense of responsibility for yourself, answer this question—"Have I been active in familiarizing myself with all of the services and facilities available to me at this college?"

Self-Orientation

Students who feel personally responsible for doing well in college seek information. They explore the college asking questions. They go beyond whatever is covered in the "orientation" program or course.

Passive and dependent students go through orientation because it is on the schedule. They expect that someone will tell them what is important to know. Often that is true. But passive learning makes others responsible for outcomes and does not lead to academic success.

If you are a new student you will probably be going through an orientation program or course. You may receive a college "Survival Kit" which tells you everything you want to know about the school and some things you don't care to know. If for some reason you are not going through an orientation program or course turn to Appendix A.

In Appendix A we have listed a variety of services and facilities your college or university probably has available to you. Take a minute now to flip through Appendix A. The Appendix will familiarize you with the college services and facilities to which an orientation program should expose you. If you have previously gone through an orientation program Appendix A will be a good review and provide you with an up-date on resource information.

Whether you use our list or the one given to you by your school, *be active* in acquainting yourself with your school. All of these services were created to help ensure your college success.

Remember: EVERY OFFICE AND SERVICE AT THE COLLEGE EXISTS IN ONE WAY OR ANOTHER TO HELP YOU GET THE COLLEGE EDUCATION THAT YOU DESIRE. Go find out about these services and take advantage of them!

If you don't get the help or information you need don't go around blaming others. Find some way to succeed! When you are successful, give yourself credit. If you fail take equal responsibility. Look carefully at the result you got, find out why, and figure out how to be more successful next time.

ACCEPT TOTAL RESPONSIBILITY FOR LEARNING

In college, consider adopting the philosophy that your instructors are responsible for no more than presenting ideas and information to you. Assume it is your responsibility to learn. Too often students are conditioned by magizines, television, and movies to be *passive.* Students expect to be entertained by textbooks and instructors. The only writings or instructors these students pay attention to are those who catch their attention. These students seem to expect instructors to compete for their attention just as professional entertainers do.

College instructors are not encouraged to become entertainers. Being an entertainer in the classroom is viewed as unprofessional at most schools. How much time and money do you think your instructors are given to prepare jokes, write funny lines, create witty sayings, come up with humorous comments, and do all the other preparation that Johnny Carson and Phyllis Diller go through? None at all.

You will be very fortunate to find an occasional instructor who not only knows the material completely but can add wit and charm to the presentation. Most instructors have much information to present to you for your consideration. Ask no more of your instructors. Instructors are simply not in the entertainment business. In fact, to become a college instructor there are no requirements to take even one course in public speaking or public presentation. If you find an instructor who is an excellent speaker and skilled at presenting information to a large audience you most likely have an unusual instructor rather than a typical one.

Consider developing the attitude that you are going to be an *active learner.* You are going to get the most out of every class. You have paid your money, so get what you've paid for. You are the consumer! You can even make a boring class interesting by assuming that every instructor has useful information for you. Be determined to learn everything you can from your instructors and textbooks.

REMEMBER THAT THE BEST INVESTMENT YOU WILL EVER MAKE IS IN YOURSELF. YOU MAY LOSE YOUR JOB OR MONEY BUT NO ONE CAN TAKE YOUR EDUCATION AWAY FROM YOU!

DEFINE SUCCESS WITH GOALS

What does success mean to you? Having a million dollars? Helping other people? Being president of a corporation? Owning a new sports car? Passing a course? Graduating from college? Holding down a job for 30 years?

All of the above could be indications of success, but not necessarily. What if the person who stayed on the job for 30 years did so because of an inability to obtain work anyplace else? What if the person with one million dollars had inherited ten million and through stupid blunders and financial mismanagement had lost most of the inheritance?

Consider defining success as: "success is reaching my goals." Using this definition as a basis, what is the first step necessary for you to experience being successful? That's right, it means you must first set a goal!

People who rarely set goals for themselves rarely experience being successful. People who don't set goals are neither successful nor unsuccessful. They are *not* successful.

A person without goals may never have thought of setting goals. Other people don't set goals for themselves because the possibility of not reaching the goals is risky. They fear failure. They try to avoid feelings of failure by not setting goals.

There are different reasons why students may not experience much success. But for many students, one of the main reasons for being average or mediocre is that they seldom set goals for themselves. As you read through this book, keep in mind that people who achieve success over and over again are people who usually:

1. Set challenging but obtainable goals that they want to reach.
2. Examine the possible blocks and barriers to reaching their goals.
3. Look for ways to get around the blocks, increase their abilities, and get help from useful resources.
4. Devise realistic and flexible plans for reaching their goals.
5. Act in ways that maximize chances of reaching their goals and minimize chances of not reaching their goals.

Every person begins from a different starting point. Every person has different goals, different strengths and weaknesses, and different barriers to overcome. Each person must follow a different route to success.

MOTIVATE YOURSELF WITH GOALS

Self-chosen goals are motivating forces. Once you establish the goals you want to accomplish, your goals give you direction. You provide an instant frame of reference for deciding what to do or not to do. When you do something that helps you move closer to your goals your brain will say, "That's right, go ahead, that's just what you want to do, that's good!"

If you don't have goals, your brain will be in a quandary. Your brain might say,

"I guess that's good, wait a minute, I'm not sure, I really can't say. What do others think? I don't know. I'm not sure what to do. Let's wait and see what happens."

A person without goals is like a ball in a pinball machine, bouncing back and forth from bumper to bumper, gradually allowing the force of gravity to determine where it ends up. Having goals is like planning a vacation trip. You know your destination. By setting goals you don't wander in a meaningless direction. Remember, however, that it is all right and quite normal to start college without definite life goals. For many students, especially those in orientation programs, a main purpose in college is to develop clear life goals.

DEVELOPING YOUR CAREER GOALS

Deciding what you want out of life and going after it can be a very strong motivating force in your life. By setting goals you give yourself purpose. There is no use being lost in the wilderness. Goals help you cut a clear path through the underbrush to the destination that you aim for.

Later on, we are going to show you in detail how to go about setting and achieving specific study goals. Right now, we ask you to focus on personal goals, on life goals. We ask you to dream a little and contemplate your college career and life in general.

Think back to those years in grade school. Do you remember the teacher or relative who thought it was a good thing to ask children, "What do you want to be when you grow up?" If you were influenced by television, movies, and story books, as most of us were, and understood that answering this question was part of the game you had to play, you probably said things like doctor, nurse, astronaut, or someone like a TV hero who popped into mind.

The reality of career goal setting is that most people who graduate from high school don't really know what they want to be. In fact, many college students don't know what they want to do after graduation. There is a better plan of attack than just seeing what careers are available about the time you graduate.

If you've entered college without a specific career you needn't get in a tizzy. A tizzy won't help you or anyone around you. Instead, think about what you want to be and where you want to go in life. You have plenty of time to make career choices. In fact, most people make four major career changes during their lives.

One resource available to you would be at the office or center that provides career counseling. The counselors can provide you with aptitude and interest tests which correlate your particular interests and inclinations with certain careers. The best thing you can do to assess career opportunities is to observe and talk to people in various occupations.

We have spent a lot of time watching and talking to happy and unhappy college students. Some students know how to motivate themselves. Others sit around griping and complaining about how unmotivated they are. If you talk to motivated students you will find that they motivate themselves by choosing and pursuing goals during their college years. In choosing goals for college, most successful students ask themselves a series of questions like these:

"What would I enjoy doing that would be worthwhile for me to do?"
"What knowledge, skill, or ability can I acquire which I will enjoy and which will provide me with income?"
"What type of person do I want to be when I leave college?"
"What courses and experiences will help me develop into the person I would like to be?"
"What interests, hobbies, or abilities do I now have that could be turned into an enjoyable occupation?"

If nothing specific is ahead of you now, then consider setting as a goal discovering what goals you'd like to have. Here's a clue to look for. A well-chosen goal

1. It excites you; you can hardly wait to get started.
2. It is definite and specific; you know exactly what it is you're aiming for.
3. It is specific and measurable; you will be able to see and evaluate your progress. It fits you well; it enables you to mesh your interests, personality, and skills.
4. It is challenging; it isn't easy to reach; it's a good test for you, and achievable.
5. Reaching it will be personally satisfying, regardless of what others may think.

People who live fulfilling lives are often future oriented. Ask around, talk to people who seem to be living life to the fullest, people who are truly enjoying themselves. We'll bet that most people you talk to of this nature are people who have in mind some future accomplishments. These are people who are oriented toward having something work better, toward learning a new skill, or toward accomplishing something that will be satisfying and rewarding.

There is nothing wrong with living for the present. But to increase the likelihood of more pleasant future moments, plan ahead and take action. You can enjoy now and work toward a good future.

DEVELOP USEFUL HABITS

Being responsible for yourself sometimes includes setting as a goal, choosing to develop better habits. You have heard talk about good study habits and poor study habits. What people are saying is that your habits determine whether or not you learn much during the time you spend studying. Two students may spend exactly the same amount of time in classes and studying, but the student with good study habits learns more and gets a better education than the student with poor study habits.

The idea behind our emphasis on habits is simply that habits either help you or

6

handicap you! People who tell us they are getting the most out of life and their time in school generally agree on the importance of developing good personal habits and good study habits.

Our goal is to help you develop habits which will make your life as a student as rewarding as possible. In the chapters that follow, we will focus on study habits that will make your life as a student much nicer. But before we do that, let's take a close and practical look at what is involved when a person sets as a goal, acquiring some new personal habits.

First, take a moment to answer this question. "If I really wanted to, could I acquire a new habit or change an old one?" Most people feel that they would be able to change a habit or acquire a new one if they truly wanted to. We recognize, however, how important it is that any effort to develop a new habit *must be self-chosen*! This means that all of our suggestions about developing useful habits are just that—they are only suggestions. Having worked with many hundreds of students at improving their ability to get the most out of their educational experiences, we know that no one succeeds at developing new habits when ordered to do so. So keep in mind that any time we suggest a useful habit take a few moments to decide whether or not it is a habit that you truly feel would benefit you.

BEN FRANKLIN'S HABIT PLAN

One of the best examples of a realistic and practical understanding of the importance of habits and how long they take to develop is found in the autobiography of Benjamin Franklin. When Franklin was in his twenties, he decided that he wanted to "achieve moral perfection." He ran into difficulties, however. Here is how he described his problem:

> I soon found I had undertaken a task of more difficulty than I had imagined. While my attention was taken up and care employed in guarding against one fault, I was often surprised by another. Habit to the advantage of inattention. Inclination was sometimes too strong for reason.

Franklin analyzed his problem and eventually concluded:

> That the mere speculative conviction that it was in our interest to be completely virtuous was not sufficient to prevent our slipping, and that the contrary habits must be broken and good ones acquired and established before we can have any dependence on a steady, uniform rectitude of conduct.

Franklin describes the plan that he worked out for acquiring useful habits. He worked on one habit at a time for one week at a time. He kept a daily record in a notebook to objectively observe his progress. His plan worked well. He reasoned that if he put constant mental effort into one desirable change for a week, the change should hold up during the next few weeks out of habit (see Chapter 12 for a more complete description of Franklin's self-improvement plan).

We want to emphasize that developing new habits is not easy. Once you have habits, however, life becomes much easier. With good study habits, you don't have to work so hard at studying. Changing old habits requires work; it takes some effort. But as William James, the great psychologist, once said, "Habit simplifies movement required to achieve a given result. It makes your efforts more accurate and diminishes fatigue." Good study habits and good personal habits will help you learn more, get a better education, and get more out of life.

As you read through the book, make a note of any habits that might be useful for you to acquire. Chapter 9 contains a "Learning Habits Checklist." The checklist will provide you with a framework for developing a plan to improve your habits.

USE PSYCHOLOGY ON YOURSELF

Once you have chosen some goals for yourself and have accepted total responsibility for your own learning, you've made a big step forward. You discover you are in charge of your mind, your life, and your future. With your sense of responsibility comes the realization that you can start using psychology on yourself. You can purposefully use psychological principles of cause and effect to influence your own development and learning.

For example, if you daydream and look around a lot in class, you can improve your concentration by using note taking techniques that encourage you to be an active and attentive learner. If you're a slow reader, you can use some of the reading techniques we suggest to increase your reading speed and comprehension. If you waste a lot of time, you can practice time management and scheduling techniques which will motivate you to spend your time in a more relaxed and productive way. If you fall asleep easily while studying, you can learn to arrange your study environment so as to improve your ability to concentrate.

Psychologists have studied the principles of learning for many years. In the next section, we describe many psychological principles and techniques you can use to improve your effectiveness as a student and at the same time give you more time for your friends, athletics, important causes, and leisure activities.

CHAPTER 2

LEARNING MORE
with
less effort

STUDY REGULARLY

Most people act as though being a successful student is different from being a successful musician with the New York Symphony or a tackle with the Pittsburgh Steelers. As any successful musician or athlete, you need to practice regularly if you want to achieve your learning goals with the greatest amount of pleasure and the least pain. Accept the fact that in college you will have to study almost every day and do more studying than you did in high school.

We suspect that the orchestra conductor would never say to the members of the orchestra, "Our next concert is three weeks away. Let's get together the night before the concert and we'll practice for seven hours." Can you imagine the football coach saying to the team, "Guys, to prepare for next Saturday's game, we'll practice 14 hours on Friday. Until then, have fun and get ready for a real workout!"

Stupid examples? Not really! The conductor and football coach know that to perform well, you've got to practice frequently for reasonable periods of time. Too much practice too late will make you a physical and psychological wreck.

Like any musician or professional athlete, you need a regular training schedule. You need a study schedule that allows you time to learn everything you need to know at a pace which helps your learning settle in and stick with you for years to come.

Some people really believe they can learn just as much by cramming all of their studying into a few intense study periods before an exam. If you believe this, ask yourself, "Can I bake a cake faster by turning the oven up to 500 degrees? Can I make a garden grow faster by constantly flooding it with water and surrounding it with heat lamps?" No. The same holds true for your learning. That's why your courses are scheduled to take several months rather than being crammed into one intensive week of study. Studying for brief periods on a regular basis will lead to better learning than if you try to cram all your studying into a couple of longer periods before an exam.

MANAGING YOUR TIME

One of your greatest aids will be to use and follow a time schedule. We rate doing this *very highly*. Start by purchasing a monthly calendar with spaces that you can fill in with important dates and obligations. Fill in dates when examinations will take place, when papers and projects are due. Marking these down helps keep you aware of what your studying is leading to. Next, fill in all the times that you plan to go to concerts, shows, family gatherings, meetings; plans for trips or other events; and so on.

After developing a picture of your major commitments for the months ahead, now you are ready to make up a weekly schedule of your classes, study hours, and other obligations. A weekly schedule gives you a clear picture of what you are doing with your time; it helps you spot an extra hour or two during the day that you can use for studying or other responsibilities. This way you can plan more free evenings to do what you want.

Follow these steps for effective scheduling:

1. Establish a well-defined and reasonable schedule, one that you can live with.
2. Budget time to prepare for each class and all examinations.
3. Budget time to take care of all of your other personal responsibilities.
4. Study course notes as soon as possible after each class period, rather than waiting until the last few days before the exam.
5. Give difficult subjects preferred times with the fewest possible interruptions and disturbances.
6. Reserve time for leisure activities and make sure that you do not study during these periods!
7. Stick to your schedule and reward yourself for having achieved your study goals in the allotted time.

A good schedule has a motivating effect. Knowing that you have an hour on Thursday morning reserved for studying, mentally prepares you to spend that hour doing the studying.

WARNING: Do not allow yourself to study too much. Schedule time for the other things that you want to do and stick to your schedule. Many students become so involved in their studying when they first start using the principles in this book they keep right on studying through their scheduled breaks. *Don't let yourself do this.* When you reach the scheduled time to stop, go get some exercise or do whatever you want to do. *Learn how to make yourself stop studying*!

Yes, you read us right. For many students, the problem is not studying too little, the problem is that they study so much they are inefficient in their studying habits.

Look at it this way. Several people have said that work expands to fill available time. You may have experienced this phenomenon in regard to a project such as cleaning up the house. Let's say that you had in mind cleaning up the house and you had three hours available on Saturday morning. If you have three hours available for cleaning up the house, it will probably take you three hours to get the job done. But let's also say that before you were able to get the job done on a Saturday morning, you received a telephone call informing you that a very important person was coming by to visit and would be there within 30 minutes. You would probably, in that circumstance, be able to clean up the house pretty much to your satisfaction in less than 30 minutes. Part of the approach that we are suggesting in this book is that you very quickly decide what has to be done, do it, and then stop.

Using a weekly study schedule such as the one that follows will show you that you have many more hours during the day than you might have ever realized. If you don't have access to a commercially prepared daily calendar with the time broken down by the hour, then go ahead and make copies of the one we have here in this book. Don't fill out your schedule right now, however; we have more to say about study periods.

HOUR	Sunday	Monday	Tuesday	Wednesday	Thursday	Friday	Saturday
7-8							
8-9							
9-10							
10-11							
11-12							
12-1							
1-2							
2-3							
3-4							
4-5							
5-6							
6-7							
7-8							
8-9							
9-10							
10-11							
11-12							

ELIMINATE DISTRACTIONS

Studying at Home

More than likely, your family, roommates, or friends have habits and attitudes that interfere with good studying. These people may have no idea that their behavior bothers you. In contrast, some people will bother you just to get your attention, especially young children.

12

While you're studying someone turns on the TV in the next room. You say, "Please don't turn on the TV, it bothers me." The person says, "I'll keep it low." Someone else walks in and wants to talk or needs to be driven to a friend's house. There is a never-ending barrage of interruptions.

So how do you create a peaceful study atmosphere with all of this craziness going on? If you are like many people, you may try to enforce some rules regarding your study time. We would suggest another approach. Here's why.

"Quiet hours" in dormitories and in people's homes are often a failure. The minute you make rules requiring people to keep noise down or leave you alone, some people seem to go out of their way to demonstrate that the rules can be broken. If you shout, scream, or demand that people keep the noise down you probably won't get the desired results. Even calm rule enforcement can lead to ruffled feathers and headaches. Rule enforcement requires time which you simply don't need to waste. If you try to enforce rules and people break them, then instead of studying you're sitting there angry, uptight, and furious at what is occurring.

There is a better approach to changing the behavior and attitudes of people around you than by making and trying to enforce rules. Whatever the interference is, first ask your friends or family for what you want. Think about what is reasonable and possible. Then ask for it. Be clear, specific, and explain in detail exactly what you would like to have from them. You may be surprised at how understanding and supporting people can be.

Remember, you may be asking the people around you to behave quite differently from what they're used to. Your friends and family's behavior isn't likely to change dramatically overnight. Be patient. Track positives. Notice and appreciate any slight improvement in the direction that you are encouraging. It's up to you to express your appreciation whenever people abide by your wishes. Be sure to express your appreciation and let the people share in your progress.

If you have a friend or family member who is not cooperative, develop a plan for yourself so that you can study and do your course work. Avoid feeling victimized. Instead, come up with a creative plan which will let you continue getting the education you want. Only use strict rule enforcement as a last resort. Remember, your aim is to minimize the amount of time and energy taken away from your real interest, that of studying and learning.

Visual Distractions

Benita is like most students. She has created a comfy nest for herself in her study area. As she closes the door to the den, the wonderful family pictures covering one wall draw her attention. Benita takes several minutes to gaze nostalgically at the photos of herself and Bill at the ocean. The next thing she knows, she's ready to pull out the slides and to heck with her studying. Walking to her desk, she spots a pile of magazines she hasn't had a chance to read. There's the TV in the corner. Why not turn it on and catch the last half of the special she wanted to watch? "I can read and watch TV at the same time," she thinks to herself. Everything in the room has a pull for Benita. She feels as though magnetic forces are drawing her to every item in the room.

And that's the trouble. Before she knows it, 20 minutes have slipped away. She glances at the clock and suddenly thinks, "Why have I wasted so much time? Okay. I'll get to work. That's the last time I'll get distracted." That's what she thinks.

As Benita returns to her studies, her mind is distracted from her notes. The family photo on the desk keeps catching her eye. The phone reminds her of several calls she has to make. She starts worrying, "If I don't make those calls tonight, I'll have real problems next week." Before she knows it, she had blown another 15 minutes rehearsing the phone calls that she should be making and daydreaming. Pictures, telephones, magazines, television programs, and such constantly distract her from her studying.

If you study at your desk, keep it cleared off. Don't go berserk and carry the principles too far. We're not suggesting you create a monastic cell with nothing but bare walls and a small light at your desk. What we're suggesting is that you sit at a desk or in a chair which is comfortable and free of articles that carry memories, free of articles that cry out, "Pick me up, play with me, use me, gaze at me."

Place your desk so that you face a wall that is void of your family history and photos. A blank wall in front of you prevents your eyes from leaving the pages of your notes or text. Place your chair so that you are not looking out a window at the passing scene. Your chair can easily face an area that will not distract you.

To reduce eye strain, your room should be well lit, with the main light source off to one side. A light directly behind or in front of you will be reflected from the glossy pages of your textbooks. A constant glare tires your eyes more quickly than indirect lighting. If you can't shift the lamp, shift your desk. Place the desk so that no portion of the bulb shines directly into your eyes. A strong light source pulls your eyes toward it. The constant strain fo trying to avoid looking at the light causes eye fatigue.

Spend a few minutes arranging your study environment. There's no use in feeling uncomfortable. The few minutes you spend will save you hours of distracted study and constant mumbling and grumbling, "I just can't get a thing done. I just can't keep my eyes on the pages. I keep thinking of a thousand other things than studying. And my eyes are killing me!" All of these distractors needn't get in your way, if you design your study area to encourage studying and not daydreaming. You need to have the best study area possible.

Auditory Distractions

As we noted, "quiet hours" rarely work as well as the rule makers hope. Distracting sounds still interrupt studying. Doors slam, phones ring, horns honk, and people move around. In fact, the quieter the study area, the more distracting these sounds become.

Steady background sounds can mask distracting noises. Play your radio or stereo softly while you study to create a steady background of "noise" to mask occasional sounds. Experiment with stations or records until you find what works best for you. FM radio stations playing instrumental music are usually best. Talk shows and fast-talking disc jockeys are usually worse for concentration than nothing at all. Some women say that turning on their hair dryers helps them to study. One student reported that he turns his radio to a place where there is no program. The static keeps him from being distracted.

Don't try to study with the television on. If you want to watch a program, then watch it. But don't try to avoid feeling guilty by having your book open to read during commercials. Studying with your television on is academic suicide. Use television time as a reward. After you have completed a successful study period, say to yourself, "I've earned a reward. I'll watch television."

Territorial Distractions

If you need to escape from distractions, GO TO YOUR FAVORITE LIBRARY! Libraries have been designed to help you succeed. People can't yell at you. Your friends can't ask you for attention. Your girlfriend can't bother you with her phone conversation. Your boyfriend won't have Monday night football blaring. Your roommate can't drag you into a conversation. Only you can prevent yourself from studying in the library. The obvious exception is the nitwit who sits across from you talking to his girlfriend or tapping his pencil. With minor exceptions, most places in a library are good for studying.

When you first go into a library to find a good spot to study, allow yourself a little warmup time. Whenever you enter a new territory, your senses are drawn to the environment. You automatically scan new surroundings. You check the walls, floor, and ceiling. You look at the lights, decorations, and furnishings. You look at the people, wonder amout certain sounds, and spend time adjusting to the feeling of a new chair. Every time you go to a new place to study, you check out the surroundings before you settle down to work. To improve your studying efficiency, pick one spot and always try to study there. Studying in the same spot will shorten your warmup time and allow you to concentrate better.

If your library is a campus social center, try to find a spot with the least amount of people traffic. Find a remote table or desk where you won't be tempted to watch all the action.

ACCEPT YOUR HUMANNESS
Concentration Span

Karen is a sophomore English major. During the summer she decided that when she came back to college she would study three hours every night without interruption. She put a sign on her door:

> Off Limits from 7 to 10 P.M.
> KEEP OUT
> THIS MEANS YOU!

Is she studying more? Yes and no. She can make her body sit at her desk for several hours at a time, but she has a problem that she hardly knows exists. While her eyes look at her book, her mind takes breaks. She sometimes reads several pages and then realizes that she has no idea of what she has read. She has been daydreaming while reading!

Does Karen need more will power? No! She needs to accept the idea that she is a human being. She needs to accept the idea that there are limitations on what the human mind can be expected to do.

The way to make studying easier is to start with what you can do now and build on that. On the average, how long can you study before your mind slips off to something else? Twenty-five minutes? Ten minutes? Most students can concentrate on a textbook 10 to 15 minutes before starting to daydream.

The next time you study, keep a note pad on your desk and notice approximately how long you can read your textbook or notes before your mind starts to daydream. Don't set any particular goals for yourself yet. First, we have to find out what is the typical amount of time you spend reading textbook material before your mind starts to wander. Let's say that you find your average concentration span is about 12 minutes. Now the question is what would you like it to be—30 minutes, 45 minutes?

Whatever goal you set for yourself, make certain you allow for your humanness. Be realistic. Set a goal that you can reach with reasonable effort and give yourself enough time to reach it. As a rough guideline, you might aim for a time span of 15 minutes by the end of your freshman year, 25 minutes in your sophomore year, 35 minutes in your junior year, and 45 minutes in your senior year. Graduate students should be able to study for about an hour without losing their concentration.

Mandatory Breaks

Once you determine your concentration span, set up your study schedule so that you take a brief break after each study segment and a long break about once an hour. If you do, you will find that you can start and return to your studies much more easily than before.

In fact, you will find the end of a study segment coming so quickly you will be tempted to continue. *Don't do it.* Keep your agreement with yourself. When you promise to take a quick break after 12 minutes, then do so. *Do not allow yourself to study more than the allotted time.*

A look at the records of most students shows why it is necessary to take these breaks even when you don't want to. With segmented study hours, studying is easier than expected, but after a while the old ways of studying creep back in.

What happens? The critical point comes when you reach the end of a study segment and find yourself so interested in the material that you decide to keep on. If you do, then your mind seems to say, "I can't trust you. You promised me a break after each 14 minutes, but after I fulfilled my part, you kept me working."

When you promise your mind a break after 12 or 14 minutes, *keep your word!* No matter how much you want to keep on, make yourself take a short break. Get up and stretch. Walk out to get a drink of water or a breath of fresh air before starting the next study segment.

Mix Study Subjects

Mark is carrying a full load in school: English, biology, chemistry, psychology, Spanish, and physical education. He studies each day at school and three evenings a week. But when he tries to recall what he has covered in an evening, he has trouble doing so.

Is Mark a slow learner? Probably not. His memory problem is caused by his study schedule. His evening study schedule looks like this:

Hour	Monday	Tuesday	Wednesday	Thursday	Friday	Saturday	Sunday
7-8		Biology	Chemistry	Spanish			
8-9		Biology	Chemistry	Spanish			
9-10		Biology	Chemistry	Spanish			

Mark's memory problem exists because he spends about three hours on one subject. When a person learns one set of facts and then goes on to learn similar facts or material, the second set will interfere with his memory of the first and the first will interfere with his memory of the second. The more similar material a person tries to learn at one time, the worse his recall will be.

How can you avoid this problem when you have lots of material to study? The best way is to mix your study hours with dissimilar material. *Do not devote all of one evening to one subject.* Switch subjects every hour or so. Always try to make your new subject as different as possible from the subject you have just finished. That way your mind can be assimilating one topic while you are reading about another. Mark did much better when he revised his schedule as follows:

Hour	Sunday	Monday	Tuesday	Wednesday	Thursday	Friday	Saturday
7-8			Chemistry	Biology	Biology		
8-9			Spanish	Spanish	Chemistry		
9-10			Biology	Chemistry	Spanish		

Although Mark's new schedule shows that he is mixing dissimilar subjects, he could apply another principle of learning. Research shows that material you memorize is retained better if immediately followed by sleep. Insightful learning can occur at any time and is not vulnerable to what follows immediately. This difference means that subjects like Spanish and chemistry tend to be remembered better if studied immediately before bedtime.

Be an Active Learner

THE FIRST LECTURE

Successful students are active in determining the requirements for each course. They use their study time to engage in behavior most likely to help them achieve course success. During the first lecture, find out answers to these key questions:

Which chapters in the textbook will be covered?
When will the exams be given?
What material will each exam cover?
What type of questions will be on the exams—essay, multiple choice?
What other work will be required?
When will the work be due?
How will the work be evaluated?
How will grading in the course be determined?
Does the instructor have an outline of the most important terms and concepts
   to be covered?
Should textbook chapters be read before lectures?
What does the instructor hope each student will understand by the end of the
   course?

These questions are a starting point. Others will occur to you as you go along. A WORD OF CAUTION: Don't make instructors feel that they are being cross-examined. Be assertive, but *tactful*. If an instructor is not prepared to answer all these questions, back off. Try to find out when the information may be available. In general, you will find that instructors enjoy answering questions about what they believe is most valuable in their courses. A few instructors may be poorly prepared, however, and could become defensive if pressed too hard.

Some instructors will have the answers to most of these questions on written handouts. If you don't receive a handout, be sure to write everything down in your notebook.

TAKE LECTURE NOTES

By writing down what the instructor says in lectures, you are helping yourself become an active listener. You are also being realistic about the nature of human memory. Human beings quickly forget most of what they hear no matter how much they would like to be able to remember.

Several days after hearing a lecture, the best that most students can do is to recall about ten percent of what was said. So, unless you tape record the lectures or alternate note taking with a friend, you need to take notes at every lecture.

Some students don't take notes. They may be trying to experiment to see whether or not they can get by without note taking. These students may have reasons for wanting everyone to know that they are not involved in the course. They may be trying to impress you with how smart they are. At any rate, if you ask a student who doesn't take notes to fill you in on something the instructor said last week, you will quickly learn for yourself how important note taking is for accurate remembering.

USE LECTURE NOTES AS A SOURCE OF EXAM QUESTIONS
AND ANSWERS

You should accustom yourself to think of your instructor's lectures as sessions which provide answers to important questions. You should actively use your notes to quiz yourself on important questions that are likely to appear on your instructor's exams.

REMEMBER: Use your notes to learn more and do better on your exams. If you remember the formula:

NOTES = EXAM QUESTIONS AND ANSWERS

you'll learn a lot, do well on your exams, and live happily ever after!

ATTEND CLASS

Attending class is such an obviously useful thing to do we're almost embarrassed to have to mention it. Yet, in a research study reported by H. C. Lindgren*, it was found that there is an important relationship between attending class and the grades you receive. A comparison of grade point averages and class attendance showed these percentages:

Class Attendance	% of Students with B Average or Higher	% of Students with C- Average or Lower
Always or almost always present	85	48
Sometimes absent	8	7
Often absent	7	45

Without speculating about underlying motives or attitudes for the moment, let's focus on behavior alone. The percentages in the table above suggest that attending class always or almost always helps to maximize your chances of success. For the student who is often absent, the percentages work in the direction of receiving low grades.

READ TO FIND QUESTIONS AND ANSWERS

Studying is not the same as reading your Sunday newspaper. Reading your textbook is not the same as casually reading a novel or light fiction. Most textbooks are not written to entertain you. You can't get away with reading only the parts of texts that interest you. When it comes to studying, you must use reading techniques which motivate you to mentally and emotionally reach out and grasp important information.

Studying can be fun, but sometimes studying is very hard work, as hard as any physical labor. Passively reading your textbooks and lecture notes over and over again is no fun and is an inefficient way to learn course material. So how do you make reading pay off? How do you read to comprehend all the important information you'll need to know?

Remember one tip! Your reading of textbooks and notes must be geared to help you prepare for doing well on tests, meeting course requirements, and developing an understanding of what you're studying.

SUCCESSFUL STUDENTS VIEW TEXTS AND NOTES AS SOURCES OF EXAM QUESTIONS! As they read, SUCCESSFUL STUDENTS LOOK FOR

*The Psychology of College Success by Henry Clay Lindgren. New York: Wiley, 1969, p. 50.

QUESTIONS AND ANSWERS THAT ARE LIKELY TO APPEAR ON THEIR EXAMS. Keep in mind, *if you are not reading and studying textbooks and notes as if you are preparing to take a test you are wasting your time*!

GUARANTEE YOUR SUCCESS ON TESTS

Here's another simple question. Have you ever taken an exam that didn't require you to answer questions? Of course not. Your grades are determined by your answers to questions, not by your pleasant personality! If instructors judged you on your personality or awarded grades because of how much they liked you, you might need to go to your local Dale Carnegie training headquarters for classes on how to win friends and influence people. To do well in college, you have to be able to answer questions posed by your instructors in class and on exams. That's why we've said that every time you read your course notes or texts, you should be looking for potential exam questions.

It makes sense that if you want to do well on your exams, you should practice taking exams. Spend your study time developing exam questions from notes and texts, then test yourself to see whether you can pass your exams.

The funny, and yet tragic, thing is that most students don't prepare for exams by taking practice tests. Most students prepare for exams by reading and re-reading their notes, texts, and other sources of information. Have you ever known an instructor who asks you to come to an exam and read your notes or textbook to him? Absolutely not! Your instructors ask you to answer questions developed from their lecture notes and the textbook.

IF YOU WANT TO LEARN A LOT AND DO WELL ON TESTS, ALWAYS STUDY AS THOUGH YOU'RE PRACTICING TO TAKE A TEST.

Pretend you are the instructor. Make up exams just like the exams you believe your instructors will give you. Get your friends to quiz you on exams they have developed. Above all, develop a realistic means of learning to pass exams. Just as orchestras rehearse for concerts and football teams play practice games, prepare for exams by taking exams.

We'll talk much more about learning to study and preparing for exams in the next chapter. For the moment, we just want you to get the "big picture" of successful learning, studying, and test taking before we go into greater detail in the next few chapters.

ACTION REVIEW:
CHECKLIST FOR LEARNING MORE WITH LESS EFFORT

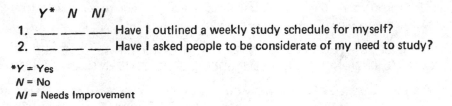

     Y*   *N*   *NI*

1. ___ ___ ___ Have I outlined a weekly study schedule for myself?
2. ___ ___ ___ Have I asked people to be considerate of my need to study?

*Y = Yes
N = No
NI = Needs Improvement

Y* N NI

3. __ __ __ Is my study free of distractions?
4. __ __ __ Do I mask distracting sounds with soft music or some other steady background noise?
5. __ __ __ Have I arranged good lighting?
6. __ __ __ Do I study in the same place each time?
7. __ __ __ Do I avoid studying one subject too long?
8. __ __ __ Have I determined my concentration span and set up study segments geared to my present ability?
9. __ __ __ Do I take short breaks after study segments and a long break each hour?
10. __ __ __ Can I distinguish between reading for interest and studying?
11. __ __ __ Do I aim my studying toward passing tests?
12. __ __ __ As I read, do I look for possible test questions and answers?
13. __ __ __ Do I take practice tests to prove how much I've learned and to prepare for examinations?
14. __ __ __ Do I always attend class?
15. __ __ __ Am I active in finding out exactly what will be expected of me during the course?
16. __ __ __ Do I have a notebook for each course and do I take good notes?
17. __ __ __ Do I view tests and notes as sources of exam questions?

CHAPTER **3**

BECOMING MORE SUCCESSFUL in your classes

© 1978 United Feature Syndicate, Inc.

What does being "intelligent" mean to you? Would you say that intelligent students have good vocabularies, are very knowledgeable, and solve problems easily? Are intelligent students able to answer their instructors' questions and get high scores on tests? If one of your goals in life is to be an "intelligent" person, then it's important for you to decide just what it is that you should know and be able to do!

Most college students believe they are intelligent people. A favorite pastime of many students and instructors is to discuss: "What is intelligence? Is it inborn? Can it be increased? Is an intelligent person creative? A wise decision maker? An independent thinker? Is there more than one kind of intelligence? If so, what different kinds are there?"

Our bias is to look for behaviors that are associated with intelligence. Most psychologists agree that an intelligent person is an efficient learner. He or she learns and remembers more than other people. But what behavior leads to this? *Asking and answering questions.* An intelligent person asks important questions and searches for the answers.

Take vocabulary for example. Most clinical psychologists believe that vocabulary is the best single indicator of intelligence. How does a person acquire a good vocabulary? By wondering, "What does that word mean?" and then finding the answer.

One good means of finding answers to vocabulary questions is to obtain a good dictionary and use it. Equally useful is to ask what people mean when they use certain terms. Search for the best words to describe something. Searching for information and answers to questions will help make you successful in school.

ASKING QUESTIONS: KEY TO EFFICIENT LEARNING AND SUCCESS IN CLASSES

If you lean back in your chair and analyze what you must do to be a successful student, it will be clear to you that you must ask and answer good questions. You must do so when writing papers, reading your texts and notes, talking in discussion groups, attending classes, and taking tests.

Think of your textbook. It consists of answers to a lot of questions. Your instructors spend much of their time developing questions to ask you in class or on tests. Think of the notes you take. Are they anything more than answers to questions? Your instructors have carefully analyzed important books, lectures, films, and other resources to generate a body of information which they present to you in class. The final task for you is to answer important questions about this information.

Let's look at simple and highly effective learning techniques developed at the University of Michigan. Several thousand students using these techniques found that once they learned to ask and answer intelligent questions they became highly successful in school. They saved hundreds of hours in studying and preparing for courses and were able to spend more time going to movies, watching television, engaging in sports activities, chatting with friends, taking weekend trips, attending concerts, and leading the "good life."

If these things interest you, then let's spend a little more time discussing how you can learn the correct techniques. One thing we promise is that you will achieve your academic goals with a great deal more pleasure and far less pain than you have known in the past. We must sound one word of caution: This goal may require you to change many of your old habits. Such changes are sometimes difficult or painful.

Why? Well, when you are used to a standard set of procedures to accomplish your goals, you often become comfortable with them and resist change. Even if you try the new study techniques, you'll have a tendency to go back to your old study behaviors. These old behaviors will help you to accomplish your goals to a degree, but with the same pain and tremendous number of hours that you have spent in the past. Once you become accustomed to the new study techniques, a lot of your old self-defeating behavior and attitudes related to studying and becoming educated will fade away. You will begin to get some good feedback from professors, friends, and yourself to indicate that the new methods save time. You will achieve your goals and have time to do things you never had time for in the past. Here we go!

PRINCIPLE I: STUDY TO PASS TESTS

Whenever you are reading from curiosity, allow your mind to go in any direction it wishes. But, when you study, *study as if you were practicing to take a test.* Practice answering questions! If you don't, you are wasting your time! Remember, it's your time, so why waste it?

PRINCIPLE II: ASK INTELLIGENT QUESTIONS

What is an intelligent question?
First, it is one that you would like answered. Second, it is framed so that in seeking the answer you will learn new and useful things. Third, it might be close to one your instructor asks on a test. Fourth, it can be a way to demonstrate what you already know.

How do you learn to ask intelligent questions?
This question itself is a good one. Practice is the answer. Practice is a useful personal habit to acquire. At first it takes some work, but later questions arise out of habit.

What will good questions help you do?
Are you and your instructor interested in the same thing? You'll only know by asking questions. You may wish to study information which is of no interest to your instructor. That's fine. But regardless of your own interests, you want to make

sure you do well in your course by knowing the information which your instructor defines as important.

If you ask good questions, you'll be able to focus on the important points of your lectures and readings. Good questions help you discriminate what your lecturers and the authors of your texts believe you should remember.

A major function of your questioning process should be to prepare you for exams. By practicing answering the questions you develop, you'll find out just how ready you really are to "ace" your exam. After all, have you ever taken an exam that wasn't composed of questions your instructor wanted you to answer? That's why we cannot overemphasize the value of proving your brilliance by answering your questions!

Not to be overlooked, you will please your instructors no end if you ask and answer good questions in class. The hundreds of hours you'll save in preparing to do well in your classes and on exams is clearly one of the hidden bonuses of the question and answer regime we're recommending.

What does a good question look like?
It usually starts with a phrase like—

> Give several examples of _____
> Which of these is an example of _____
> Describe the function of _____
> What is significant about _____
> List the important _____
> Compare and contrast _____
> Interpret the following _____
> What is the structure of _____
> Identify the following _____
> Why does _____

GENERATE INTELLIGENT QUESTIONS

How can I determine what the important questions are?
Pretend that you are the instructor, and generate questions from your texts, lecture notes, and old exams. Think of questions before you go to class, and then listen to see whether or not other students ask the same questions or whether or not the instructor supplies answers to those questions.

Write out questions for a lecture or an assignment. Then ask your instructor whether or not he thinks these questions are important and what other questions you should attempt to answer.

Do not be afraid to ask your instructor what he or she thinks are the important questions!

Most instructors are happy to tell you what they think is important. Give them a chance, and they'll take a mile!

Ask your professor what goals he has for the students in his class. If you want a clear answer, you must learn to ask questions that help him to clarify for himself the questions he would like the class members to answer. You might ask—

"What should a student be able to do and what important questions should he be able to answer after having completed this chapter (unit, training, program)?"

"What important questions do you think we should be looking at in this unit (chapter, assignment)?"

"Can you suggest particular articles or books that highlight the issues we will be be discussing in this unit?"

"What important things should we be looking for in this particular reading (film, case study)?"

Such questions should be asked in as positive a manner as possible. Students have a tendency to put instructors on the defensive. It is your job to ask an instructor in what direction the course is headed and to reward him for telling you. A comment like, "Thanks, that really clarifies things for me" is something an instructor appreciates and will increase the likelihood that you won't have to ask next time.

Now that I know what intelligent questions are, what is the best way to get into the habit of developing questions and answers?
We prefer to start by showing you how you can get a lot more out of your reading by turning it into a question-answering process. We'll then get into note taking, test taking, and a variety of other important study skills, but reading is the most important, so that's where we'll begin!

READING = QUESTION ANSWERING

Increasing Your Reading Speed and Comprehension in Textbooks

One of the fastest ways to spend less time reading assignments is to learn how to figure out the important questions and answers as quickly as possible. First, you should know that a large percentage (perhaps as many as 80 percent) of the words you read are redundant. Most words simply link ideas. The ideas are the answers to the questions you wish to answer.

Second, you already know much of what you have to comprehend. As you survey and read, what you want are the answers to questions that you generate or find in the chapter. Dozens of studies with college students show that the following steps will increase your reading speed, comprehension and memory:

READING CHAPTERS IN TEXTBOOKS

Survey—Question—Read—Recite—Write—Review = The SQ4R Method

Remember, improved comprehension is the ability to answer more questions from reading assignments. This approach to reading is considered by many experts on study skills and reading improvement to be the most efficient and effective means for getting the most out of reading material in the least time. The primary concern of students using this method will be to *ask* and *answer* intelligent questions as they read.

What you should do is described in the following sections.

Survey and Question

The goal of surveying is to determine what important questions are answered in the textbook chapter. First, go to the beginning and end of the chapter to see whether or not there are chapter objectives, a list of questions, or a chapter summary. If so, read them right away! This is where you will find the important points that authors wish to stress and the questions students should be able to answer after completing the chapter.

If you can answer the questions and already know what is in the summary or chapter objectives, you probably won't have to read the chapter. But don't decide yet. If there is a set of questions, a list of objectives, or a chapter summary, you're ahead of the game; if not, you soon will be.

How do you survey? *The process of surveying involves quickly skimming the chapter to determine what important questions it answers.* Look for titles, subtitles, illustrations, pictures, charts, lead sentences in paragraphs, and questions that will give you a basic idea of what the chapter is about.

While surveying it is easy to turn titles, subtitles, and lead sentences into questions. For instance, "Communist Techniques of Brainwashing" is a paragraph heading in *Understanding Human Behavior*, a textbook written by James McConnell. You simply turn it into "What were the techniques of brainwashing used by the Communists?"

By generating questions as you survey, you keep yourself alert to the important points in the chapter. Reading becomes an active, goal-oriented process. As you survey, you should formulate questions that, when answered, will give you a good summary of the chapter. *The result of your survey will be a list of questions.*

To prove your brilliance, you may wish to attempt to answer the questions you have generated in your survey before reading. This attempt serves to tell you how much you already know before spending an exorbitant amount of time reading. Many students are amazed at their ability to answer a large percentage of the questions they have formulated in their survey.

Another helpful technique is to quickly summarize what you already know about the chapter. By talking to yourself about the chapter, you help yourself to focus on the important questions you should be able to answer after having read it.

Read to Answer Questions

It is now time to read: Read as quickly as you can. Read to find the answers to questions you have generated while surveying the chapter and to find new answers that you haven't predicted while surveying.

Remember: In many instances, your questions and answers will be summarized in titles, subtitles, or lead sentences. Occasionally, you may have to read beyond the headings for more important details. But not with the regularity that caused you to waste a lot of time in the past when you were looking for unimportant details.

When reading to answer questions, you learn to predict important questions before spending a lot of time reading. You learn to read selectively. You read to find answers to questions. When you come to the answer to a question that you hadn't predicted, you simply slow down, formulate the question, and make sure you know the answer. When you come to material you already know, keep on going to find out what you don't know.

Recite and Write Answers and Summaries

Now that you have (1) read to answer the questions from your survey and (2) developed new questions and answers that you hadn't predicted, it is important for you to go one step further.

Recite and write the answers to the questions that you developed while surveying and reading. Equally important, *recite and write a short summary of what you have just read.* These procedures are excellent means of proving to yourself that you have asked and answered the important questions from each chapter.

Practice talking to yourself (even if people think you're a little crazy) about the answers to your questions. Often students rush on to a new chapter before thoroughly proving to themselves that they are familiar with the contents of the chapter they just read. They say to themselves, "I read it. I know what it's about." DON'T MAKE THAT MISTAKE! Prove to yourself by answering questions and writing chapter summaries that you really do comprehend the chapter.

Review

If you have followed the steps so far, you are in excellent shape to review the chapter at any time. You will have a set of questions and answers representing the contents of the chapter. When preparing for your exam, quiz yourself on these questions until you feel comfortable that you could give accurate answers to them if they were to appear on your exam.

We also suggest summarizing to yourself, orally or in writing, the contents of the chapter and comparing your summary with the one you wrote after having read the chapter.

Taken together, these activities will really give you the feeling that you've mastered the material. When you know you can answer questions correctly and make accurate summaries, you will be more confident that you have mastered the chapter. You will spend less time attempting to re-read chapters and otherwise involving yourself in a variety of superstitious and time-consuming study activities which seldom help you to ask and answer important questions.

The Result

You have now

1. Surveyed the chapter.
2. Generated questions.
3. Read selectively to answer the questions in greater detail.
4. Found questions and answers that you hadn't predicted.
5. Recited and written answers to questions and chapter summaries.
6. Reviewed the chapter by practicing answering questions and summarizing the chapter.

You now have a good understanding of the chapter.

TAKE THIS BOOK, FOR EXAMPLE

For an example of how to use SQ4R, look at how this book is organized. "About This Book" gave you an outline of the contents. Next, in "How to Use This Book," we urged you to rapidly skim through the book to answer questions about it. Now you are reading the book in greater detail and talking over the new things you are learning with your orientation class or with your study partners.

At the end of most chapters you find an "Action Review." The review questions help you specifically determine whether or not you are putting into practice what you are learning. Later in Chapter 9 you will find a comprehensive checklist for reviewing what you've learned and applied up to that point about being more successful in college.

In other words, we wrote this book in a way which helps you put into practice what we know works for students!

Why should I believe that this approach works?
Evidence collected at the University of Michigan Reading Improvement Service and other learning centers has shown that most good students use these techniques. When poor students learn SQ4R they raise their grades, reduce study time significantly, increase reading speed, and improve comprehension of textbooks.

Advantages of SQ4R

With SQ4R, you spend less time memorizing facts that you will soon forget. You don't waste time reading and looking for things you already know. Your preparation for tests is a continual process. By the time you take the test, you will find that you have answered most of the questions. You focus on grasping the key concepts. Details are then much easier to remember. You don't waste time looking for details that are unimportant to you or your instructor. You learn to take an expert's point of view and to think things out for yourself. You learn to sit down and generate answers that you didn't think you knew. You then search for additional information, which makes polished answers out of incomplete ones. You learn to organize and structure your studying. You state your goals as questions, seek answers, achieve your goals, and move on.

Difficulties of SQ4R

It is difficult to change old study patterns. You may be accustomed to reading every word, always afraid that you're going to miss something. A new technique such as the SQ4R Method may appear reckless because you learn so fast. It takes more energy to ask questions and generate summaries than it does to let your eyes passively read printed pages. It is easier just to open a book and start reading. You study a little bit frequently instead of waiting until the end of the course and cramming.

How can you reconcile advantages and disadvantages? There are advantages and disadvantages to *everything!* This is true for both successful and unsuccessful students. If there were no disadvantages, if it were easy, then everyone would be more successful. There are costs, but once you are into SQ4R, the gains are worthwhile.

Imagine yourself agreeing to run in a 10 kilometer race several months from now. You will be running with friends and it is important for all of you to do well. To be at your best, would you loaf around until the last few days and then prepare by running day and night until the time of the race? No. You'd start now with a weekly schedule of jogging and running. A little bit of practice on a regular basis prepares you the best. The same approach is true for effective studying and remembering.

Try the study techniques, and look for results like the following:

The quality of your questions and answers will improve with practice.

The amount of time it takes you to generate questions and summaries will decrease.

The amount of time it takes to verify and improve your answers will decrease with practice.

You will be able to cover large amounts of material in far less time.

You will find that you are producing the same questions as your instructors, textbooks, and friends.

With practice, you will find that the summaries you generate come closer to those of the author.

These techniques are based on several well-established learning principles. First, when you learn material under conditions that are similar to those under which you will be tested, there is a greater likelihood that you will remember it. People learn meaningful material faster than they memorize unrelated or nonsense information. Learning new material is easier when you associate it with familiar material.

The SQ4R Method sounds helpful, but could I start by just using parts of the technique or using the whole technique on small sections of my work?
Our students report best results when they begin practicing the entire technique at once. But some people will adjust best to the SQ4R strategy by practicing on a small section of work to see immediate results. They gradually increase the use of this method as they become more comfortable with it.

PREDICTING EXAM QUESTIONS

How do I go about predicting exam questions from sources other than my text?
Once you accept the value of always studying as if you were practicing to take a test, you'll be on the right track. It is important to gear your study behavior to collecting questions and answers that you expect to find on your exams. By using the reading techniques that we have suggested, you will have a good start. Your reading will always be geared to asking and answering important questions.

In addition to this style of reading, there are several other techniques that will help you to collect a good set of exam questions. Note taking, asking friends and instructors, collecting old exams, holding discussion groups, and using textbook and student manual questions are several that we suggest. Let's start with note taking.

SOURCES OF EXAM QUESTIONS
Lecture Notes

Think of your lectures as textbook chapters. Each usually has a main theme and makes several important points. If you listen for them, they will be easier to hear.

We encourage you to take lecture notes in outline form. This habit will help you to focus on the main points that can be turned into questions. Your job is to record these questions and to make sure that you know how your instructor would answer them.

Most good instructors answer their questions thoroughly in class, but sometimes they only allude to the answers. Wise students always make sure they know what questions the instructor believes are important. They then go to outside sources if more information is needed than has been supplied in the lecture.

Here are the steps we suggest you follow in taking lecture notes:

TIPS ON TAKING NOTES

Use large pages for taking notes. Put the date on each day's notes. Use an outline form whenever possible. The most commonly used outline form is this:

I. (Roman numerals for major topics)
    A. (Capital letters for major subgroups)
        1. (Numbers for supporting examples, people, points)
        2.
    B.
        1.
            a. (small letters for supporting details)
            b.
            c.
        2.
        3.

Write down complete phrases and statements, rather than single words. Underline points the instructor gives special emphasis to. Put the notes from each class on separate pages. Keep a different notebook for each course. Write your name, address, and phone number in each notebook.

1. During the lecture, take notes on the right-hand side of the paper. Leave a margin on the left.
2. After the lecture, take several minutes to turn your outline into test questions. The main theme and subtopics can be turned into questions. Usually each lecture will supply you with three to seven good exam questions. They should be written in the left-hand margin.
3. At least once a week, review the questions you have asked. Pretend that you are taking a test. Give yourself an oral quiz, or, even better, practice by taking a written quiz. Then compare your answers to those given in your notes or textbook.

Remember: This procedure will help to make something meaningful out of lectures that often leave you in a quandary. Your purpose is to go to lectures looking for questions and their answers. If you come out of each lecture with several questions and answers, you'll be pleased. They're likely to be on your next test!

Your notes may not look as neat as those below. We don't expect you to carry a typewriter to class. If your notes are neat and as close to outlined as possible, you'll have a much better chance of turning them into a good set of questions. These notes were taken at an introductory psychology lecture. The topic was hypnosis, and the notes represent a portion of the total lecture.

Questions
                            VII. Hypnosis Oct. 26th
                                A. Anton Mesmer
                                    1. Cures by magnetism—capture magnetic fluids from planets to cure sickness

What is a placebo?

How did Mesmer bring about the "grand crisis" in his patients and what was the effect?

What are some of the reasons people gave for the effects of Mesmerism?

Why was Mesmerism banned in Paris?

Why did Charcot believe some patients could be hypnotized more readily than others

What effect did studying hypnosis have on Freud's view of mental illness? (important!)

2. Put magnets over patients to cure them
3. Cures due to *placebo effect*—power of suggestion
4. Mesmer's Grand Crisis
   a. Mesmer dressed in robes like wizard
   b. Patients in tubs of magnetized water
   c. Patients went into trance-like states
   d. *Mesmer had discovered hypnosis*
   e. Mesmer urged patients to go into "grand crisis"—like convulsive seizure
   f. Mesmer was convinced that "grand crisis" was responsible for cures of patients
   g. *Mesmerism* was name given to *technique for inducing trance state* and the "grand crisis"
   h. French government investigated Mesmer—and said it was a hoax—cures due to suggestion and imagination rather than magnetism
   i. *Mesmerism was banned* in France on moral as well as medical grounds and Mesmer retired to town outside of Paris

B. Early uses of hypnosis to study mental disorders
   1. Name is taken from *Greek word for sleep*
   2. Jean Charcot said there was a close *connection between hysteria and hypnosis* and that only hysterics could be hypnotized
   3. French scientists rejected Charcot's claim and insisted that hypnosis was a result of suggestibility
   4. Freud and hypnosis
      a. Studied under Charcot—after his studies he began to think of mental illness as being due to psychological rather than physiological causes
      b. Freud used hypnosis to suggest to

What new technique did the use of hypnosis lead Freud to develop?

patients that their symptoms could disappear—this worked sometimes, but they often recurred

c. Freud found that only patients who experienced a strong personal trust in him could be hypnotized daily

d. *Freud renounced hypnosis* as a therapeutic tool and *developed the technique of free association.*

Old Exams

Students often feel guilty when they admit to having looked over past exams. They feel that they have been cheating. Our answer to this is bunk! Looking at old exams tells you what an instructor thinks is important information for which students should be responsible.

Looking at old exams doesn't guarantee that you'll know exactly what your exam questions will be. Instructors change their lectures, textbooks, films, guest speakers, and even their opinions once in a while. Consequently, exams change from semester to semester.

Nevertheless, by looking at old exams you may answer several important questions:

1. Does the instructor have some favorite questions that he asks every year?
2. Do test questions appear to be taken from material similar to that which you are studying?
3. Do test questions come primarily from lecture notes or from a variety of sources?
4. What types of questions does the instructor prefer: multiple-choice, short-answer, true-false, essay?
5. On which content areas does the instructor place the most emphasis?

These questions should help you see the value of reading and taking notes in the question-answer format. There is no guarantee that the instructor will take most of the questions from the same source that he used in years past. Yet it is surprising how similar questions are from year to year regardless of the textbooks that instructors use. They often chose new textbooks that give better answers to the same questions they have been asking for many years. Equally important, few instructors make drastic changes in their course notes from semester to semester. They usually only update them. The questions you generate from course notes, textbooks, and other sources, combined with old exam questions, will be invaluable in your exam preparation.

Textbooks

Always read the questions that precede or follow the chapter. Such questions are included by authors because they believe that students should be able to answer them after having read the chapter.

Many instructors take their test questions directly from those in the textbook. Surprisingly, many students never look at these questions. They seem to feel that no one could be so stupid as to tell them exactly what they should be able to do after reading the chapter.

Authors usually try to help students, not trick them! If you are not in the habit of answering chapter questions, we recommend you use them as the starting point in your effort to organize a good set of questions and answers.

Student Manuals

Always use student manuals that accompany many textbooks as sources of exam questions. Student manuals have been designed to inform you of the study behaviors that will be helpful to students using the textbook. Manuals often contain true-false, multiple-choice, fill-in, and short essay questions. Even if your exam is likely to be made up of questions that differ in style from questions found in the student manual, the manual questions are still valuable.

You only have to change the manual questions into the style likely to be found on your next exam. Don't avoid student manuals that are in a programmed format. Student manuals are designed to save you time. Whatever the format of the student manual, use the manual as a source of exam questions. The time you save by using a student manual can be used for other important activities, like watching television or taking a nap.

Note: *The publisher of your textbook may have a student manual available even if the instructor did not require its use.* Check this out—especially for introductory textbooks. If a student manual exists, you can purchase it through the bookstore or directly from the publisher. Sales figures from textbook publishers show that 7 out of 10 students using textbooks do *not* purchase and use the accompanying student manual.

Discussion Groups and Friends

Some of the best sources of test questions, yet often the most overlooked, are friends and fellow students. By talking with other students enrolled in the course or with students who have been enrolled in past semesters, you can formulate an excellent perspective of the types of questions and answers you should be looking for. Just as important is finding out what you might avoid.

Many students believe it's difficult to organize formal study groups. Some students simply have a preference for working on their own. This strategy can be self-defeating. By organizing the questions and answers from a variety of sources, you are in an excellent position to compare yours with those of fellow students.

We compare this process with the pastime of trading cards. You collect as many as you can and simply trade off your extras to build up an even stronger set. Similarly, you find out what questions other students feel are important. You compare your answers to theirs to ensure that you haven't overlooked important information. Everyone comes out stronger than when he entered the game. Everyone is better prepared to ask and answer intelligent questions.

By studying in a group or with one other person, you will help to ensure that you

1. Structure a situation in which other people will encourage you to involve yourself in the study activities we have recommended.
2. Ask and answer questions that you believe are important and are likely to be found on your next exam.
3. Find questions that you yourself hadn't predicted.
4. Refine your answers with additional information supplied by other students.
5. Put together practice tests.
6. Take practice tests.
7. Develop a more efficient and effective process of preparing for exams.

Instructors

At the risk of sounding bold, we suggest that your instructor is the best source of information on forthcoming test questions. Many students find it difficult to ask instructors what they believe is important. As we suggested earlier, most instructors are happy to tell you what they think is important. Give them a chance: Ask them!

Ask your instructor: "Could you specify the areas in which we should concentrate our studying?" "Are there particular topics which you feel we should devote more time to than others?"

Whatever you do, *don't* ask: "Are there any areas you feel are unimportant?" "Which of these chapters should we avoid, considering all that we have to study for this test?" If you ask such questions the instructors may be so peeved they will assign the encyclopedia. Most instructors believe that everything they teach is important. In trying to determine what is likely to be on exams, your goal is simply to persuade instructors to narrow down all the important things they have told you to a precise statement of what your exam will look like. If you are pleasant and thank your instructors for their help, you'll be way ahead of the game. You may even find out the exact format of the exam and which questions are most important.

THE RESULT

Predicting exam questions is the most useful technique we have found in preparing students to learn the important concepts covered in their courses. Equally important, it helps them to pass their exams with much greater ease. If you have followed our suggestions, you will have collected exam questions from

1. Your textbook chapters.
2. Your lecture notes.
3. Old exams.
4. Lists of questions in your textbooks.
5. Lists of questions in student manuals.
6. Discussion groups and friends.
7. Your instructor.
8. Lists of chapter objectives.

Once you have collected a good set of test questions, you will be better prepared to follow through with the procedures we shall suggest in the next section
on tests.

*Is the purpose of education to learn how to answer instructors' questions and pass
tests?*
Yes and no! If you want to understand the experts and even go beyond them it is
important to be able to ask and answer the same questions that they believe are
important. If you're realistic, you know you have to pass the requirements of the
course. If you understand what your instructor wants, then you will learn a lot. If
your instructor is less than adequate, then it is a matter of meeting his criteria and
going on to better courses. There is no need to waste a lot of time in the process.

*How can developing questions for class help me if I'm afraid of being called on in
class?*
By preparing questions and answers and having practiced, you will be less afraid. It
is natural to be scared if you are not prepared. Talk to yourself about the answers
to questions your instructors are likely to ask in class. Once you have proven to
yourself that you know the answers, you will be less fearful about your ability to
answer similar questions in class. Language labs and discussion groups are useful
places to begin to practice answering questions your instructors might ask in class.
If the fear comes from a general fear of having everyone look at you when you
talk, go see what is available on campus in the way of assertiveness workshops or
classes in verbal communications. If you ask around you will find that there are
some instructors who are very good at helping shy people become more comfortable speaking in groups.

GETTING STARTED DEVELOPING QUESTIONS AND ANSWERS

It is best to begin by practicing, predicting, and answering exam questions! Each
week, count those questions and answers that you have collected from textbook
reading, old exams, lecture notes, student manuals, discussion groups, classmates,

and your instructors. To monitor how well you are doing, record the number of questions and answers you have for each class.

ACTION REVIEW:
CHECKLIST FOR SUCCESSFUL STUDYING

Here is a list of guidelines that will help you to monitor your studying and your success at implementing the learning strategies we've described.

Y* N NI

1. __ __ __ Do I, out of habit, use the SQ4R method for learning course material?
2. __ __ __ Do I survey the reading first, ask questions, and then read to answer questions?
3. __ __ __ Do I practice writing answers to questions and write chapter summaries?
4. __ __ __ Do I generate questions from lectures, textbooks, chapter summaries, student manuals, old tests, discussion groups, and chapter objectives?
5. __ __ __ Have I asked my instructor what goals he or she has for the students in class?
6. __ __ __ Do I keep a weekly record of the number of questions and answers I generate for each class?

*Y = Yes
N = No
NI = Needs Improvement

CHAPTER 4

Doing well
ON TESTS

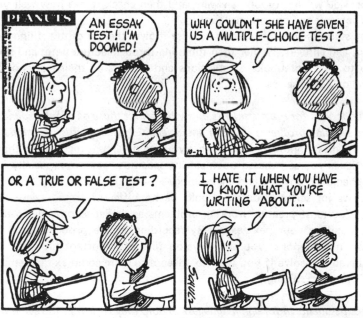

© 1970 United Feature Syndicate, Inc.

PREPARING FOR TESTS

Now that I have collected a good set of questions and answers, how can I make sure that I'll do well on the tests?
Periodically, go through the questions you have generated to see whether or not you can still answer them. Avoid saying to yourself, "I know the answer to that one." Prove to yourself how brilliant you have become! *Orally and in writing, practice answering your questions.*

Review and Test

Using the questions you have collected, make up practice tests. Take practice tests under conditions as close as possible to actual test conditions. Then compare your answers with those you have generated from your textbooks, lectures, and so on.

Quiz Yourself

Here are some specific hints about making and taking practice tests, strategies for taking tests, and other useful exam preparation techniques.

When you quiz yourself orally from your notebook, cover up your answers with a blank sheet of paper. After answering your question orally, remove the paper and check to see how accurately you have answered your question. If you use cards, place your questions on one side and your answers on the other.

This system will allow you to quiz yourself quickly by looking at your questions, provide written or oral answers, and then check to see how well your quiz answers compare to your original answers.

Most students like this system because it gives them a central filing system of questions and answers. Rather than fumbling through lecture notes and textbooks, they go to their notebooks of questions and answers or their stacks of question cards and quiz themselves.

That sounds great for most students, but what about those of us who spend most of our time working problems in math and science? How can this technique help us?
One of the most important insights that you can develop is recognition that success in a particular course is based upon solving specific problems, especially in mathematics, chemistry, physics, and engineering.

Reviews for science courses should be no different from reviews for other courses. You must practice working problems as similar as possible to those that will be found on your next exam. By recording sample problems on 4 X 6-inch cards, or in notebooks, you will develop files of important problems that you should be able to solve if you wish to advance to more complex mathematical and scientific problem solving.

How about students in foreign languages? Should they review in the same way?
Yes, all students should review by practicing answering the important questions

that are likely to appear on their next tests. Language students must maintain basic vocabulary and grammatical skills if they wish to develop more complex language skills. By reviewing these areas, language students assure themselves of continued involvement in the basics upon which more complex skills are built.

Making and Taking Practice Tests

Practicing the exact behavior you will be required to perform in a test situation not only prepares you to do well, it also helps you to relax and build your confidence. After successfully passing practice tests, you are less likely to feel the uneasiness and tension about tests that may have accompanied your old study routines. You will know you have studied the right questions, and you'll sleep better for knowing you've studied correctly. Here is how to make and take practice tests:

1. Determine the amount of time you'll be given to take your instructor's exam; take practice tests over the same length of time. Taking tests under realistic time pressure is important. If you force yourself to do so, you'll feel more comfortable when you're in the actual testing situation.
2. Arrange the questions you've been accumulating from chapters, lecture notes, study groups, old exams, and other sources into practice tests.
3. Try to put the questions into the same format that the test will offer (multiple-choice, short essay, and so on). Old tests will give you a good idea of the format your instructor is likely to use.
4. Take your practice tests under conditions as similar as possible to those under which you'll be tested. The classroom in which you'll be tested is the best place to take practice tests. If it is not available to you, make sure you practice in a room where you won't be bothered.
5. Try to answer your questions without referring to your books or other sources of information.
6. When attempting to answer questions for which you need more information, try to guess and make up things as if you were in a real testing situation, trying to earn at least partial credit. This procedure forces you to take what you already know and to determine what might be the answer, rather than saying, "I just don't know!"

   Yes, this approach is known as "bulling," and it often makes the difference between an A and a B! Bulling is writing out an answer that makes sense to you, even though you don't remember exactly what was said in the textbook or lecture. You often know more than you think. An imaginative answer can be a good way to demonstrate your comprehension.
7. Once you have completed the test, compare your answers with those that you have in your own set of questions and answers. Use your textbooks and notes to refine your answers.
8. After noting the questions you have answered well and those in need of improvement design a new test. Follow the same procedure that we have outlined in steps 1-7. Take the new test and continue repeating the steps

41

until you think you have mastered all the questions and answers likely to appear on your instructor's test.

Weekly and Final Practice Tests

When you take weekly practice tests in each subject area, you'll find that exam panic and last minute cramming are a thing of the past. Before each scheduled test, take a comprehensive practice test made up of sample questions from your weekly tests. You'll be pleasantly surprised at how much easier it is to pass your final practice test when you have been taking weekly tests.

Taking weekly tests allows you to master small amounts of information each week and then to put everything together in a final practice test just before you take the real thing.

The Advantages of Preparation Strategies

But isn't this strategy very time consuming?
It may appear so, but students who collect test questions and answers, take weekly practice tests (or quizzes), and take final practice tests spend far less time on irrelevant and wasteful studying. These students practice exactly what their instructors will require of them, "asking and answering intelligent questions."

Such students also obtain a more solid education. They remember what they have learned much better than students who "cram" for exams. The research into forgetting, done originally by Ebbinghaus and replicated many times over, shows that people quickly forget most of what they learn unless they review and rehearse the material.

We have assumed in our suggested study techniques that you want to pass tests well and obtain an excellent education. Your success in life after college is a function of what you can do, not of your grades. When you go to an attorney to have a contract drawn up, do you ask "What grade did you receive in contract law?" Or, if you have a pulled muscle, do you ask the physician about his or her scores on anatomy tests? No. You seek help or services on the basis of what people know and can do.

To obtain learning that lasts each of us must apply the basic principles of learning. Otherwise, we end up with average grades but little knowledge.

TAKING YOUR INSTRUCTORS' TESTS

Now that you know how to prepare for a test, let's make sure that you know how to relax and use your time wisely once you have the real test in your hands.

General Rules

1. Read the instructions to determine the types of questions you'll be expected to answer. Determine where you'll earn the most points. Don't spend a lot

42

of time reading; just form a basic idea of how the test is set up, and plan your attack.

2. Divide your time to ensure that you schedule enough for all portions of the test. Otherwise, you'll devote too much time to the most difficult parts and wind up "choking" when you find that you won't be able to complete the whole test.

3. Before starting, determine whether or not answering the easier questions will earn you just as many points as answering the more difficult questions. If so, complete the easy questions first. After answering them you'll have more confidence, and you will be able to pass on to the more difficult questions.

4. Make sure you understand what each question is asking. If the directions say, "Give several examples of. . . ," then do exactly that! Give instructors exactly what they ask for. Don't twist questions around into something else.

5. If you don't understand a question or find it extremely difficult, place an X by it, and move on to easier questions. You can come back later. This procedure saves time and prevents anxiety. Most important, you may find the answer hidden in other questions as you move through the test. Don't waste precious time trying to dig out the answers from the back of your brain. Expect the answer to come to you as you work on other items, just as you do when trying to recall a person's name. Relaxing and expecting the name to come to you in a few moments works better than struggling to remember.

Written Examinations

Written examinations tend to be of two types, long essays and short answer tests. Long essay examinations ask you to "Trace the development of . . ." or "Explain and provide supporting evidence for each of the theoretical views. . . ." At most schools an essay examination will require you to write from five to ten essays. (Note: If the instructor indicates that it is a Blue Book examination, this means you must purchase from the bookstore and bring to class a book with a blue cover designed specifically for writing examination essays.)

Answering Long Essay Questions

OUTLINE ANSWERS
Outline your answer to an essay question before writing it. In this way you will ensure that you include key ideas for which you will earn points from the grader. The procedure saves time in the long run. You can organize your answer and can be sure to include everything that is important. You will feel more organized when you begin to write and will have few uncertainties about whether you have included everything you should.

INTRODUCTION
Begin with several paragraphs that ask the most important questions or present

the main ideas of your answer. It can help to pretend that you are writing a short article and need an interesting opening.

DEFINE TERMS

Define the terms that you use in your answer. Be sure to call attention to conflicting viewpoints or any uncertainties in your mind about the question asked. This approach often clarifies for the instructor why you have answered the question in a particular manner.

USE SUBHEADINGS AND EXAMPLES

As you write, be sure to use subheadings for longer answers. Subheadings show you and the reader the organization in your answer. It is crucial to use examples to support your main points. You demonstrate that you really know what you are talking about if you can present examples to substantiate your position.

CONCLUSIONS

Summarize and draw conclusions. Be definite and positive. But note, do not include any new data, points, or examples in the conclusion! Add new questions, perhaps, but no new information.

POLISH ANSWERS

Above all, write legibly! After you have finished writing, pretend that you are the grader. Ask yourself, "Have I misread or misinterpreted the questions? What did I leave out? Have I made any careless mistakes?" Allot time at the end to polish your answers, add necessary points, and deal with more difficult questions that have puzzled you.

Short Answer Tests

Short answer tests may contain from 20 to 40 items worth from one to eight points each. Such tests may ask you to

Define each of the terms and concepts in a list
Outline an experiment or study
List the main points in favor of a procedure
Give three criticisms against _____
Draw and correctly label a chart, graph, or structure (for example, a nerve cell)
Summarize the views of an author or scientist
Name the basic steps or stages in a process

Most of your answers on short answer tests will be incomplete sentences and phrases. Long paragraphs continuing on the back side of the page are not what the instructor asked for. For ease in grading most instructors appreciate clear, legible, easily read lists of phrases. Use the back of the exam for jotting down some of the lists and other information you have memorized.

44

Answering Objective Questions

Never, never leave an answer blank, unless there is a penalty for guessing. If there is a penalty, guess only when you can eliminate at least half the possible options, two options where there are four in a multiple-choice question, for example.

Read objective questions carefully, but answer them quickly. If the answer is not immediately obvious to you check off a tentative answer and come back to it. Later items in the test often give clues to the answers in earlier items.

Contrary to the popular advice about never changing answers, *it can be to your advantage to change answers.* The research evidence shows that when students have prepared well for an examination the number of students who gain by changing answers is significantly greater than the number of students who lose by changing answers. Be cautious about changing answers. But your second thought, if you have prepared well, may be more valuable than following a simple rule which is largely a myth.

ANSWERING MULTIPLE-CHOICE QUESTIONS

As you answer multiple-choice questions, always be sure to eliminate the obviously incorrect answers first. You will save considerable time and will help to reduce anxiety about choosing the correct answer.

Read and answer each question quickly. Look for key words and phrases such as "Which is *not* . . ." or "*According to* Skinner . . ." or "The *strongest* evidence. . . ." After you have answered all questions, go back and check to see that you have read them correctly. If you have time, reread them all. If not, reread those that you marked with X the first time through because you were unsure of your answers.

ANSWERING MATCHING QUESTIONS

Check to make sure you have read the directions for matching questions carefully. Sometimes students believe that matches are so obvious that they do exactly the opposite of what is asked. If the instructions say, "Match those that are different" or "Match those that are opposite," you'll feel rather foolish if you have spent a lot of time matching those that are similar.

A real time saver is answering the easy ones first. This tactic reduces the chance of guessing incorrectly on more difficult matches.

ANSWERING TRUE-FALSE QUESTIONS

Never waste a lot of time pondering true-false questions. Many students have been known to waste major portions of test periods attempting to "solve" true-false questions as if they were Chinese puzzles. If an answer isn't immediately apparent, don't become frustrated. Simply move on to the next question. Just one or two questions aren't worth that many points. They don't deserve the precious time that could be devoted to other, more important questions. The points you miss on a true-false question may be recalled later in an essay question through a shrewd use of your imagination, called "bulling."

QUESTIONS YOU DIDN'T THINK YOU COULD ANSWER

Students are often amazed when we ask them to try answering questions and writing summaries after simply surveying a chapter. They say, "But I haven't read it yet!" Students then go ahead, do it, and find that their answers and summaries are fairly accurate, sometimes close to perfect. How do humans remember what they didn't know they know? Stored in your brain, you have much information of which you are unaware. When you force yourself to come up with answers, you'll be amazed at how much you know!

We want you to remain humble, but we want you to be able to pull yourself out of jams by being creative. Go ahead and answer questions to which you have no immediate answers.

What can you do when you come to a question that baffles you? Try to remember that in your reading you're likely to have picked up some information that is relevant. Put down anything and you're likely to earn a few points, which is more than you'll have if you leave the answer blank. While taking the exam, you're likely to pick up some information related to the answer you need. If you can't figure out the exact answer, you can probably figure out an approximation. In math, for example, you may work out problems and come up with incorrect answers. You may not receive complete credit, but partial credit is surely better than a big zero.

Using your imagination takes practice and even a little confidence. It is not the most important study skill that we can recommend, but using your imagination can be valuable at times.

You Can Write Comments About the Test

If, in spite of all your excellent preparation you are still a bit nervous about the test, then try imagining that written across the top of the test is the statement, "Feel free to write comments about the test items."

Wilbert J. McKeachie, known for his research on ways to improve teaching, discovered that when this statement was printed at the top of tests, many students did better. The students who were helped most were those who had stronger than average fears of failing. An interesting result was that it didn't matter whether students actually wrote anything about the test or not! Just the presence of the statement was enough to improve the scores of students who had strong fears of failing.*

So, when you are taking a test, remember that you should *feel free to write comments about the test items!* If you believe that a question is poorly worded, then say so. But *also* go on to explain why and perhaps suggest a better wording. The whole purpose of the examination is to show that you know something about the subject. *Note:* If you have doubts about the instructor's allowing comments on the questions, then go ask!

*"Relieving Anxiety in Classroom Examinations" by W. J. McKeachie, Donald Pollie, Joseph Speisman. *Journal of Abnormal and Social Psychology*, Vol. 50, No. 1, January 1955, pp. 93–98.

Ask Questions During the Exam

Instructors know that their questions are not always clear. Sometimes the wording isn't as accurate as it should be. That's why most instructors will answer questions about text questions during exams.

Take advantage of this willingness. If there are one or two questions that just don't make sense, go ask the instructor such questions as, "I'm not sure when this material was covered. Could you give me some help?" "I saw all the films but don't remember the one that this was covered in; can you give me any clues?" "Where was this information presented in the textbook?" "The way this item is worded, there are several possible answers, this one and this one. Which do you want?"

If you are drawing a blank anyway, you have nothing to lose by seeing whether or not the instructor will give you some hints. He or she will not give you the answer, but a comment like "That item is from the chart at the end of Chapter 6" may give you the clue you need. Try asking. Asking the instructor for clues can be worth several extra points on every exam.

The Advantages of these Test-Taking Strategies

The strategies described in this chapter can improve your confidence by encouraging you to attach your tests in a reasonable and predictable manner. By using these techniques, you should achieve more points on any given test.

When taking tests, you will find that you don't make those stupid mistakes which make you want to kick yourself and ask, "Why didn't I use my brain?" You will read the questions carefully, plan your time well, determine the value of specific questions, and answer questions in ways likely to earn the maximum number of points. You will engage in test-taking behaviors that we most often observe in students who comprehend their course material and do well on exams. In essence, you will be a more successful student and will still have time for friends!

Again we emphasize that students who use these techniques *seldom*

1. Misread the test questions and answer questions incorrectly.
2. Waste time on questions that stump them.
3. Waste time answering questions with information they know is irrelevant.
4. Run out of time and fail to complete the test.
5. Lose points as a consequence of changing their answers at the last minute.
6. Have difficulty answering questions that require them to "bull" a little.
7. Develop exam panic when a test appears more difficult than they had predicted.
8. Fail tests (they usually receive B or better).

Students who use these techniques report that they

1. Get better grades on tests.
2. Receive more points for answers than they would have predicted.

3. Feel more relaxed and confident while taking tests.
4. Feel confident that they haven't wasted their time while answering complex as well as simple questions.
5. Feel better organized while taking tests.
6. Seldom leave out important information from answers.
7. Are able to complete exams in the allotted time.
8. Get higher grades in their courses.

One Final Tip

It is not necessary to play the "suffering student" game. Learning can be pleasant. Studying for exams can be efficient if you use the principles we've just discussed. If you prepare well for exams, then the night before each exam you can relax and do one more very helpful thing: GET A GOOD NIGHT'S SLEEP!

ACTION REVIEW:
CHECKLIST FOR SUCCESS IN PREPARING FOR AND TAKING TESTS

    Y *   *N* *NI*

1. ___ ___ ___   Do I practice quizzing myself on possible test questions?
2. ___ ___ ___   Do I make up and take practice tests?
3. ___ ___ ___   Do I practice taking tests under conditions as similar as possible to those under which I will be tested?
4. ___ ___ ___   When I take tests, do I use the techniques suggested in this chapter?

*Y = Yes
 N = No
 NI = Needs Improvement

CHAPTER 5

WRITING effective papers

Using your library well

© 1965 United Feature Syndicate, Inc.

WRITING PAPERS FOR INSTRUCTORS

The successful way to write papers closely parallels the steps you take in preparing for and taking tests. Begin by asking the following question when writing a paper for an instructor: "What important questions should I answer in this paper?"

For students willing to approach writing from this perspective, we have found the process to be less difficult and less time consuming. More important, their papers are precise, accurate, and well received by instructors. Here are the steps to follow in planning and preparing your papers.

Pick Your Topic

Pick the topic you find most interesting! Try to make it a topic that your instructor believes is important. By listening closely in class, you will often detect certain interest areas that are the instructor's favorites. Our students have found it best to choose topics that they and their instructors have enjoyed doing research on and reading about.

Instructors can supply bibliographies and other information about their favorite subjects. It may be helpful to talk with them after class or to make appointments to discuss your planned paper. Talking with the instructor will give you added insights on the advisability of writing in specific areas. It is also a good way to get to know your instructor.

When you have an assigned paper to write, our suggestion is that you prepare in advance, by selecting at least three possible topics. Have a preferred topic, of course, but have several alternative topics that you would find interesting in case the first one proves to be unworkable. Make an appointment to talk with your instructor about your proposed topics. If you ask good questions during your discussion with the instructor, it is amazing how often the instructor will suggest many approaches, useful ideas, and key concepts to include which will almost outline how your paper should be written. During this discussion, your instructor can also warn you about certain problems to avoid and which issues are either too simple or too complicated to attempt in your paper.

Remember Your Audience

Always keep in mind that you are writing to an audience of one person, your instructor. You are not writing an article for the Saturday Review or for your school paper. You are not writing a paper which will be published as an article in a professional journal. Because your instructor is the person whom you are writing for, it is very important to take extra time to find out exactly what you need to do in your paper to get a good evaluation. If your instructor is vague or unwilling to talk with you about what you plan for your paper, talk to students who have taken the course in the past and try to read papers that other students have written for this instructor to gain an idea about what he liked and disliked.

Ask Your Questions

Ask yourself, "What important questions should I answer in the paper if I wish to cover the topic adequately?" This attitude will help you determine whether your topic is too broad or too narrow. Too often students find that they would have to produce encyclopedias to cover all relevant questions adequately. If you limit yourself to a few important questions, you will be in a better position to relax as you do the research and writing.

Begin your paper by indicating that you intend to deal only with specific questions. Be humble and indicate that you recognize that there may be other significant questions, but that you have chosen to limit yourself to several high priority questions.

What if my instructor says that I have missed the important question? What do I do then?
This possibility is why we stress talking with your instructor to determine whether or not the questions that you think are important are those that the instructor would like answered.

What if I'm in a class of 200 and don't have access to the instructor or teaching assistant?
You have several alternatives. Many schools provide students with a writing skills center. If you put into practice the recommendation in Chapter 1 about acquainting yourself with your campus you should know where writing help is available. Take advantage of this useful *free* service! It is there for all writers no matter what level they are at.

Go to the library. Find a *reference librarian*. Reference librarians are wonderful people to know. They can help you find sources of information you probably wouldn't think of. They know the library thoroughly and can be extremely helpful. Use them. That is what they are paid for.

Skim through the most recent books and journals that deal with your topic. Even new books can be several years behind the times, so it is wise to go to journals that are more up to date. By looking at what the experts are doing, you are likely to get a better idea of the important questions currently being investigated.

Discuss your topic with students majoring in the subject. They may be aware of important questions that you have overlooked.

Once you have a list of good questions, the next step is to search for some answers. The best place to search for answers is usually back at the library.

HOW TO USE YOUR LIBRARY WELL

Libraries are wonderful places. In libraries you can discover extraordinary ideas, amazing information, and new worlds. You can find facts to support impressions you have, or data which disproves opinions you don't like. To have these experiences, it is highly important to know how to use a library.

Card Catalog and Microfiche

The card catalog is where you start in search of answers to your questions. In many libraries the card catalog is being converted to a microfiche system. Microfiche is a piece of photographic film usually 4 X 6 inches. It contains information greatly reduced in size so it has to be magnified for reading. One microfiche sheet replaces dozens of card catalogs. It saves space, is cheaper to produce, and can be updated quickly. To use the microfiche, you sit down at a magnifier, insert the card, and find the items you are looking for.

Let's say your paper is going to be about nutrition and athletic performance. You've heard about high protein diets, carbohydrate loading and seen ads for Gatorade. You've heard about professional athletes on vegetarian diets and seen Bruce Jenner praising Wheaties. Hou do you find out what the facts are?

With your questions in mind, you'll probably want to start with the subject index. Libraries index their books in three ways: by *author, subject,* and *title.*

Use your imagination when looking through the subject index. Look under every topic you can think of—nutrition, dieting, physical education, health science, and so on. Make notes of book titles and authors, and always write down the complete call number of the book. The call number is the library's code number which tells you exactly where the book is shelved.

If a book has the statement "reference" or "reference desk" you will not find the book in the open shelves. An instructor has probably placed the book on reserve so that no one can check it out of the library. If you go to the reference desk, they will probably let you have the book for several hours and in some cases, days. At some libraries you can check a reference book out at closing time if you return it promptly first thing in the morning.

Periodical Index

After looking through the card catalog and microfiche, step over to where the library lists all of the periodicals it subscribes to. Most of your up-to-date information, especially scientific reports on research, appears in professional journals long before it is reported in books. Flip through the lists, looking for titles of journals which could contain articles related to your topic. For your paper you'd cover all the nutrition and physical education journals.

The journals of national professional groups are often titled *The American . . .* or *National Society of . . .* or *The Journal of the American. . . .* So be sure to look under "American," "National," and "Journal" in the alphabetical listings.

As you record call numbers for books and the journals you will begin to see a pattern. The books and journals with relevant information are clustered in two or three places in the library. Now, by going to these sections, you will discover other books and journals that you didn't see in the catalog indexes.

Start in wherever you choose. Read first to get a general orientation. When you find useful data or passages you may want to quote in your paper, be very accurate in your recording. It can be very frustrating later when back at your typewriter if you can't remember which author you quoted, or if the statement in your notes is one of your own observations rather than being a quote obtained from an author. Most libraries have coin operated photocopying equipment available. Save time by using it.

From the journal articles you will learn which authors are most highly regarded and most frequently cited as experts, and will get clues about books to look for. Some professional journals publish book reviews of the latest books. You may learn about a book before the library purchases it. In such cases you may have to go to instructors in that area to see if any one of them has purchased the book and will allow you to borrow it.

From the books you will learn about which journals focus on your topic most frequently. You may learn about an older journal article that is exactly what you are after. You may discover, for example, that several articles on blood sugar and endurance have been published in medical journals. Thus, you have another area of information open up to you.

Reference Section

You still haven't used your library well, however, if you ignore a third source of useful information. It is the reference section. In the reference section you will find many resources, such as encyclopedias. Of most interest right now, however, is the *Reader's Guide to Periodical Literature.*

This index lists in alphabetical order the titles of articles published in the major popular magazines. If an article on nutrition and athletic performance has appeared in *Time Magazine, Saturday Review, Psychology Today, Sports Illustrated,* or *Runner's World,* the *Reader's Guide* will list it. Some physicians and scientific researchers publish directly in popular publications so don't discount magazines as a source of information. Besides, the information is usually easier to understand than in professional journals and books.

Use Other Libraries

Don't overlook other libraries in your area. Sometimes city or county libraries have books which the college libraries do not have. Other colleges in your area may have references which you cannot find in your own library on campus. You can use any library nearby, even the medical school library if there happens to be one in your vicinity. These other libraries may not allow you to check books out, but there is no problem in walking in and using any materials they have.

You'll soon discover that having the questions in mind that you want to answer, you can quickly cut through the massive amount of material that could otherwise distract you. By reading to answer your questions, you save precious hours that might otherwise be lost in meandering around, wondering how much you should include in your paper.

Write Your Answers

Now that you've gathered your information, it is time to write the answers to your questions.

Write the answers to your questions as precisely as possible. Be brief. Don't include irrelevant information that clouds the issue. Make your point, back it with sufficient examples and data, and leave it at that. Answers to questions are more believable when they are precise and well documented. Let your reader know that you've done research on the answers.* Quote experts in the field. The more authoritative your examples, the better you will be able to convince your reader, but don't overdo it. Several good examples are all that you need to prove your point.

Brief accurate quotations are more effective in supporting your points than lengthy quotations or your statements about what other people have said. Brief quotations, figures, and specific facts are more persuasive than vague generalizations.

Arrange Your Answers

Once you have written your answers, arrange them in order so that they build upon one another. Your next task is to connect them by writing the minimum amount of material between each answer. These transitions from answer to answer should be brief. Upon completion of the transitions, you will have written the first draft of your paper.

The Steps So Far

1. Determine which questions you will answer in your paper.
2. Write an introduction describing the intent of your paper and the questions that you will answer.
3. Answer each question as precisely and authoritatively as possible. Provide examples to support your position.
4. Document your sources in footnotes and a bibliography.
5. Put your answers in sequence so that they build upon one another.
6. Provide transitions from answer to answer.

Rewrite Your Paper

After you write your first draft, make an appointment to go over it with your instructor. Most instructors are willing to help you and will give you good feedback about whether you are ready for the typewriter or need to do more research.

Important: Give precise references to your information sources in footnotes and in your bibliography. Provide all the information a reader needs to go to the specific publication and find the exact pages referenced.

Revising is where the real writing of any paper takes place. Most writers produce several rough drafts before attempting their final version. Plan from the beginning to produce a rough draft which you will then revise into your final copy. This way you can produce your first rough draft much more quickly and won't be wasting time going back trying to edit, correct typing mistakes, and such as you write out or type your first draft.

When you are in a position to rewrite your paper, you should

1. Have your instructor look over your rough draft.
2. Make sure you have clearly indicated which questions you will answer.
3. Check to see that your transitions flow smoothly from answer to answer.
4. Vary the length of your sentences. Most of the writing in journals and research books is composed of long, involved, complicated sentences. Such sentences are typical of the way that academics think and talk. Long sentences do not make interesing reading, however. On the other hand, you don't want to make your writing style too simple. The best approach is to mix both long and short sentences.
5. Correct any grammatical, punctuation, or spelling errors.
6. Rewrite or refine any answers.
7. Finish the paper with concluding comments and remarks. *Include in this section statements about what you learned in the process of writing the paper.* State why writing the paper was a valuable experience for you. Also include any questions, if any, that writing this paper has raised in your mind.

Good Effort and Learning

The grade given for a paper is influenced by three questions in the back of the instructor's mind:

1. Did the student put good effort into this paper or was it written with the minimum possible effort?
2. Did the student learn anything or is this paper just a collection of words?
3. Is the paper original or has it been plagiarized?

If you can arrange to do so, glance through a large number of papers. Certain quick impressions will begin to emerge. Some students turn in papers that show very little effort. You don't have to be an instructor to see that such students are trying to get away with the absolute minimum commitment of time, effort, and involvement.

INSTRUCTOR REACTION: Disgust
STUDENT LEARNING: None
GRADE: D to C–

Some students do more work, but they lack involvement with the topic. Their approach is to check out all the books they can on the subject, sit down the night before the paper is due, and put together lists of quotations: "In 1937, C. S. Johnson said . . . . His view was criticized by Smith who said . . . , by Brown who said . . . , by Jones who said. . . . But then in Eggland's 1949 book. . . ."

INSTRUCTOR REACTION: Ho-hum, a collection of secondhand ideas
STUDENT LEARNING: Minimal, shows no thinking
GRADE: C to B–

Once in awhile, a student will copy long passages from a book or article and will turn in the paper without mentioning the author's name or the source. Does this approach succeed? Rarely. An article written by an expert on a subject is not like a paper written by a student who is attempting to learn a subject. And, frankly, most instructors can spot the style and point of view in the paper as having come from a certain author.

INSTRUCTOR REACTION: Plagiarism
STUDENT LEARNING: Zero, tried to cheat
GRADE: F

It's human nature to consider taking shortcuts, but some efforts to save time involve high risks. The probability is high that the payoff will be the opposite of what is desired. That's why asking and answering questions works so well. An instructor reading your paper can see that your work is *original,* that you put *good effort* into it, and that you have *learned* something. Remember, an experienced instructor will usually be able to recognize exactly what you do or don't do in preparing your paper.

Grammar, Spelling, and Neatness

One final set of suggestions is important. Determine whether your instructor requires that papers be typed. You can safely assume that the instructor prefers it, most instructors do. If you can't type, consider taking a typing class. In any case, typing is easy to learn and it is one of the best investments you can make in self-improvement. (*Note:* Your school may offer a credit course in typing. If so, you can not only learn a valuable skill but you may even earn credit toward your degree as well!)

Hand-written papers are difficult to read. They slow the instructor down and cause eye strain. Your instructor reads hundreds of articles, books, and papers every year. It is a sign of consideration to present your writing in the easiest possible readable form. Make your typed copy as professional as possible. Use clean white paper, double space the lines, and make a minimum number of corrections on the typed copy.

Always be careful to follow any directions your instructor gives for footnotes, bibliographies, references, or other requirements. There is nothing worse than devoting hours to a paper only to have it returned as incomplete. The consequences of failing to follow directions can be costly.

It can be a pain in the neck to follow the requirements assigned by your instructors. It may be one of the small sacrifices you have to make as a student. You may be dismayed to find that what your instructor wants for the form of a paper contradicts what your English instructor taught you to do. In the end, however, you'll probably find out that there's a good reason for your instructor's request. Go along with the suggestions and you will usually be better off, both in the grade you receive and the level of your blood pressure after completing the paper.

Above all, make sure that your spelling is accurate. Use a dictionary whenever you are in doubt. If you find that you have serious problems in this area, you will be wise to make an arrangement with someone to check your paper for spelling and grammatical mistakes. Regardless of the quality of your ideas, there are few things that bother instructors more than poor spelling and bad grammar.

It has been shown in several studies that instructors usually grade papers higher when the papers are neat and clean and when they include good spelling and good grammar. *A word to the wise:* Look sharp, at least on paper.

Note: Always keep a copy of your paper. The original could get damaged or lost. Some instructors keep papers. Play it safe. Make a copy for yourself before turning in the original.

ACTION REVIEW:
CHECKLIST FOR SUCCESS IN WRITING PAPERS
AND USING YOUR LIBRARY

Y* N NI

1. ___ ___ ___ Do I write papers using the question and answer format?
2. ___ ___ ___ Have I asked the reference librarian for suggestions about where to look for information?
3. ___ ___ ___ Do I use the card catalog and microfiche to track down good reference sources?
4. ___ ___ ___ Do I get up to date information from professional journals?
5. ___ ___ ___ Do I use the *Reader's Guide* to learn about useful magazine articles?
6. ___ ___ ___ Do I use other libraries in the vicinity?
7. ___ ___ ___ Are my quotes and references accurate?
8. ___ ___ ___ When the rough draft is completed, do I ask the instructor to look it over and give me suggestions for improvement?
9. ___ ___ ___ Do I check to insure that my grammar and spelling are correct?
10. ___ ___ ___ Is my written work clean and readable?

*Y = Yes; N = No; NI = Needs Improvement

SUGGESTED READING

Strunk, William, Jr., and E. B. White, *The Elements of Style* (New York: MacMillan, 1972). This book can be valuable to any person wanting to improve the quality and clarity of their written communications. Buy a copy and hang onto it. This little book is the best book in print on how to use good grammar, punctuate correctly, and write clearly.

Turabian, Kate L., *Student's Guide for Writing College Papers,* 3rd ed. (Chicago: University of Chicago Press, 1976).

CHAPTER 6

SETTING
and achieving
your study goals

© United Feature Syndicate, Inc.

HOW TO SET GOALS

Why should I set detailed study goals?

You need goals so that you will know where you're going in the process of educating yourself. When you know what you want to achieve, you can set your mind to it, achieve it, and stop worrying about whether or not you'll do well in your courses. Setting goals is one of the strongest ways of motivating yourself to study efficiently and effectively.

Students who don't set specific study goals are usually uncertain about when they are going to do what they have to do in order to pass their courses. If you can determine what you should study to pass a course and set up a schedule to achieve study goals, you'll be in good shape. The last several chapters have covered study skills. Now let's make sure you know how to set study goals and design a schedule to achieve your goals.

How do I figure out what my study goals should be?

First, you have to ask, "Who or what can tell me what I have to do to pass the course?" The best sources of information are usually

1. Your instructor.
2. Assigned course materials.
3. Course outlines.
4. Course schedules.
5. Other students.
6. Class discussions.
7. Student manuals and programs.

From these sources you will usually be able to tell what important tasks you have to accomplish in order to achieve your goal of passing a course and becoming a more intelligent person.

What types of tasks are usually required of students who wish to pass courses?

1. Passing tests.
2. Passing quizzes.
3. Writing papers.
4. Participating in class discussions and presentations.
5. Completing projects.

What should I consider when scheduling my study tasks?

In addition to knowing the types of tasks that you must accomplish, you should know *how, when,* and *where* they should be accomplished.

How do I accomplish these tasks?

If through some twist of fate you've skipped the study skills chapters, please go back and read them. They were written in order to teach you study skills that will help you to accomplish these tasks effectively. Now we'd like to show you how to define tasks and to set schedules that will help you to achieve your course goals.

What questions should I ask when defining tasks and setting up my study schedule?

When must the tasks be completed?

How much time do I have to complete the tasks?

How much can I reasonably expect to accomplish between now and the time the tasks are due?

How can I divide up my studying so that I don't put everything off until the end?

How much should I do each day if I wish to accomplish my tasks on schedule?

Are there specific requirements for the completion of tasks—format, number of pages, references, and so on?

Where will I be required to demonstrate accomplishment of the tasks?

After answering these questions, you'll be better equipped to design an effective schedule for completing tasks. You will know where you are going, how you will get there, and how to recognize when you've arrived.

SCHEDULING TASKS TO ACHIEVE YOUR GOALS

The process of scheduling is quite simple:

1. Determine your goal.
2. Figure out what study tasks you have to perform to achieve your goal and how much time you'll have in which to complete them.
3. Plan to spend specific study periods completing your study tasks.
4. Use a checklist or graph to record your progress as you complete your tasks.

Here's how to set up a schedule to achieve a goal. We shall use a model in which the student's goal is to pass an exam. Having read the study skills chapters of this book, our student decides that the best way to achieve this goal is to use the technique of collecting and answering questions that are likely to be on her next exam. Here are the steps we suggest that she follow in scheduling and completing tasks that will lead to her goal.

Steps in Scheduling

Goal: To receive a passing grade on the next test.

Task 1: Determine when and where the next test will be and what material it will cover.

Task 2: Determine the sources of test questions (textbook chapters, lecture notes, study groups, old tests, student manuals, and so on).

Task 3: Determine how many chapters must be read between now and the test.

Task 4: Plan to read a specific number of chapters each week and to generate questions from them.

Task 5: Plan to spend specific study periods each week generating test questions from course notes, old tests, discussion groups, friends, student manuals, and so on.

Task 6: Plan to spend specific study periods each week making and taking practice tests.

Task 7: Design checklists or graphs to record progress in collecting questions and answers, as well as taking practice tests.

USES OF RECORDING PROGRESS

Keep Yourself on Schedule

What's the purpose of using a checklist or graph to record my progress in completing tasks?

Checklists and graphs are probably the most effective means of keeping you consciously aware of taking the actions that will lead to your goal. You define the tasks that you plan to accomplish, determine when you'll have time to complete them, record when each task is completed, and reward yourself for completing the task on schedule. That's not so hard, and it will have a tremendous motivating effect on your performance.

Reduce Anxiety and Forgetfulness

We have found that when students keep checklists or graphs, they have less anxiety about whether or not they're studying frequently enough. They find that after establishing a schedule, they're more likely to study and complete tasks. Graphs and checklists serve as reminders of what must be done and when it must be accomplished.

Record and Reward Your Progress

An important suggestion that we make to you when using a checklist or graph is that you reward yourself for being at places on time and accomplishing specific tasks. Our goal is to help you to establish reasonable goals and to accomplish your goals. Using graphs or checklists is the best means by which you will be able to record your progress. Checklists and graphs will remind you of your responsibilities and accomplishments. Checklists and graphs say to you, "This is what you have to do today," or "Congratulations for having accomplished _____."

Few students fall by the wayside when they have clear means of establishing goals and of recording and rewarding their progress, provided that they know how to study. If you reward yourself for completing tasks, you'll find that you are more likely to achieve your goal.

DEVELOPING CHECKLISTS

What should I include on my checklist?
Each checklist should tell you

1. What tasks should be accomplished.
2. When each task should be accomplished.
3. On what date you actually accomplished each task.
4. Whether or not you rewarded yourself for accomplishing each task.
5. Whether or not you achieved your overall goal.

Important Steps in Developing a Checklist

1. Specify each of the tasks that you must accomplish to achieve your overall goal.
2. Arrange the tasks in order of importance and according to when each is most easily accomplished.
3. Indicate next to each task when you expect to achieve it.
4. Record next to each task the actual date it has been completed.
5. Record next to each task the reward you will give yourself for having accomplished this task.
6. Record whether or not you have rewarded yourself for having accomplished the task on time.
7. Record whether or not you have rewarded yourself for having accomplished the overall goal.

What would a checklist look like for the student whose goal is passing her next test? Here is an example of what was worked up with one student who wished to pass her test.

Beverly Bailey

Introductory Psychology

Goal: To receive a passing grade on first psychology test of the semester.

Exam date: September 29, 1981

Today's Date: September 1, 1981

Responsibilities: Read Chapters 1-5 in *Understanding Human Behavior: An Introduction to Psychology* by James V. McConnell

Take lecture notes for September 1, 3, 5, 8, 10, 12, 15, 17, 19, 22, 24, 26
Get a copy of last year's exam
Attend study group

Study Behavior	Due Date	Date Completed	Reward	Yes/No
1. Read Chapter 1, and generate questions, answers, and summary	Sept. 2			
2. Read Chapter 2 (same as 1)	Sept. 5			
3. Read Chapter 3 (same as 1)	Sept. 9			
4. Read Chapter 4 (same as 1)	Sept. 16			
5. Read Chapter 5 (same as 1)	Sept. 23			
6. Generate questions from today's lecture and take practice quiz	Sept. 1			
7. Same as 6	Sept. 3			
8. Same as 6	Sept. 5			
9. Same as 6	Sept. 8			
10. Same as 6	Sept. 10			
11. Same as 6	Sept. 12			
12. Same as 6	Sept. 15			
13. Same as 6	Sept. 17			
14. Same as 6	Sept. 19			
15. Same as 6	Sept. 22			
16. Same as 6	Sept. 24			
17. Same as 6	Sept. 26			
18. Generate questions from old test	Sept. 10			
19. Make up and take practice test for Chapters 1, 2	Sept. 7			
20. Make up and take practice test for Chapters 3, 4	Sept. 17			
21. Make up and take practice test for Chapter 5	Sept. 24			

Study Behavior	Due Date	Date Completed	Reward	Yes/No
22. Make up and take practice test from all sources of questions	Sept. 27 28			
23. Meet with study group to make up practice test	arrange			
24. Take exam	Sept. 29			
25. Achieve goal: Pass Exam				

Beverly decided to reward herself each time she completed one of her tasks on time. She set due dates, then recorded when each task was completed and whether or not she had received her reward. It was important for her to list her rewards so that there was something to motivate her to complete her tasks on time. Too often in the past, she had found that she put everything off until the last minute and became panic stricken when she realized how much she had to do. Now, whenever she completed a task on time, she wrote "Yes" on the chart, indicating that she had rewarded herself for doing so.

Beverly listed a series of rewards to choose from whenever she completed a task on time. She was free to choose rewards from outside the list, but we encouraged her to develop a list that would motivate her to keep up with her studies.

Beverly's Reward List

1. Going for a walk
2. Reading magazine
3. Eating snack
4. Taking a nap
5. Playing cards
6. Watching television
7. Playing tennis
8. Calling boyfriend
9. Going on date
10. Ice-cream sundae
11. Riding bike
12. Going to a show

Beverly's list of rewards is likely quite different from one you would develop. Perhaps your list would include a back massage or playing Space Invaders. Remember, everyone works for rewards that he or she values. We encourage you to reward yourself for studying effectively, just as most people reward themselves for going to work by collecting pay checks.

Isn't it rather time consuming to make checklists? Couldn't the time be better spent by studying?
The checklist took Beverly three minutes to make up. Once it was completed she know what she had to do and when she had to complete each task. Afterward, she spent less time worrying about whether or not she was doing the right things and whether she was ahead of or behind schedule. The checklist was an excellent investment in the game of learning to study efficiently and effectively. You may use any type of checklist you wish. This one is simply a model with which our students have had much success.

Benefits of Developing a Checklist

What can you guarantee the checklist will do for Beverly?
The checklist of specific things to do is very helpful. If you have everything written out in an organized fashion, it is easy to refer to. You can see what needs to be done more easily. You won't be overwhelmed by the amount of information you need to learn. Also, you are much less likely to be surprised by an important test or paper.

If Beverly follows the behaviors that she outlined she will, first, have a good set of questions, answers, and summaries for each chapter. Second, she will not be faced with the problem of having put off reading the chapters until just before the exam. She will study the chapters periodically over a month and will finish them at least a week before the test. Third, she will make up questions and answers immediately following her lectures and will practice quizzing herself to prove that she really comprehends the lectures.

Fourth, Beverly will take a practice test for each chapter before she takes a final practice test. Before the exam she will be well prepared and will have spent less time in final review. This change has a tremendous positive effect on most students' digestive tracts and fingernails. Stomachs and fingers often take a beating when students wait until the last minute to figure out what will be on the next exam.

Fifth, Beverly will find out from her friends what they think will most likely be on the exam. Sixth, she will also obtain a fair idea of what will be on this year's test from looking at a copy of last year's exam. Seventh, she will be constantly reminded whether she was ahead of, keeping up with, or behind her study schedule. Eighth, she will reward herself for completing each of the tasks leading to her goal of passing the exam.

Finally, Beverly will increase her motivation to study. In fact, in talking to us about this schedule, she became so enthusiastic that she was going to do the first two chapters immediately to get a head start. We suggested to her, however: "Don't let yourself jump ahead; only allow yourself to study for a certain amount of time. When you've finished, reward yourself, and go on to something else."

The Completed Checklist

It is interesting to compare the proposed checklist that Beverly had made out at the beginning of the month with the same checklist after she had attempted to follow her schedule of tasks and to reward herself for completing the tasks on time. As you will see, she chose most of her rewards from her original list. Periodically she satisfied a whim or spur-of-the-moment desire that she hadn't included on her original list of rewards. It is important to notice that she did not have to spend a lot of money to reward herself. By choosing activities that she enjoyed but seldom found time for when going to school, she was able to encourage and reward her good study behavior while keeping herself out of debt.

Many students ask, "But what can I reward myself with? Everything costs so much." Yet students often complain that they never have time to do things they enjoy—playing cards, watching television, riding their bikes, drinking beer, and going out with their friends to enjoy the "good life." Scheduling rewards for completing tasks encourages students to partake of their favorite activities. They have no reason to feel guilty, as so many students do when they take time away from their studies. The rule of thumb is *when you earn a reward for studying, take it, and never, never, cheat yourself.*

Study Behavior	Due Date	Date Completed	Reward	Yes/No
1. Read Chapter 1, and generate questions, answers, and summary	Sept. 2	*Sept. 2*	*Hour TV*	*Yes*
2. Read Chapter 2 (same as 1)	Sept. 5	*Sept. 5*	*Hour TV*	*Yes*
3. Read Chapter 3 (same as 1)	Sept. 9	*Sept. 9*	*Read mags.*	*Yes*
4. Read Chapter 4 (same as 1)	Sept. 16	*Sept. 16*	*Sundae*	*Yes*
5. Read Chapter 5 (same as 1)	Sept. 23	*Sept. 23*	*Hour TV*	*Yes*
6. Generate questions from today's lecture and take practice quiz	Sept. 1	*Sept. 1*	*Hour nap*	*Yes*
7. Same as 6 *(late)*	Sept. 3	*Sept. 4*	*None*	*No*
8. Same as 6	Sept. 5	*Sept. 5*	*Cards*	*Yes*
9. Same as 6	Sept. 8	*Sept. 8*	*Rode bike*	*Yes*
10. Same as 6 *(late)*	Sept. 10	*Sept. 11*	*None*	*No*
11. Same as 6	Sept. 12	*Sept. 12*	*Ice cream*	*Yes*
12. Same as 6 *(late)*	Sept. 15	*Sept. 16*	*None*	*No*
13. Same as 6	Sept. 17	*Sept. 17*	*Tennis*	*Yes*
14. Same as 6	Sept. 19	*Sept. 19*	*Walk*	*Yes*
15. Same as 6	Sept. 22	*Sept. 22*	*Cards*	*Yes*
16. Same as 6	Sept. 24	*Sept. 24*	*Call friend*	*Yes*
17. Same as 6	Sept. 26	*Sept. 26*	*Hour TV*	*Yes*
18. Generate questions from old test	Sept. 10	*Sept. 10*	*Sundae*	*Yes*
19. Make up and take practice test for Chapters 1, 2	Sept. 7	*Sept. 7*	*Show*	*Yes*
20. Make up and take practice test for Chapters 3, 4	Sept. 17	*Sept. 17*	*Show*	*Yes*

Study Behavior	Due Date	Date Completed	Reward	Yes/No
21. Make up and take practice test for Chapter 5	Sept. 24	*Sept. 24*	*Show*	*Yes*
22. Make up and take practice test from all sources of questions	Sept. 27 28	*Sept. 27, 28*	*3 hours TV*	*Yes*
23. Meet with study group to make up practice test	arrange	*Sept. 27*	*Nap*	*Yes*
24. Take exam	Sept. 29	*Sept. 29*	*Date*	*Yes*
25. Achieve goal: Pass Exam	*Exam Grade*	*92%*	*Concert*	*Yes*

Beverly's Completed Checklist

Notice that Beverly failed on several occasions to complete her tasks on time. Therefore, she did not reward herself. It was important that she receive the reward only when the task has been completed on time, for procrastination had been a big problem for her in the past. She decided it was important that her chart serve as a means of encouraging her not only to complete her work but also to complete work on time.

For other students, punctuality may not be a problem. It would not be necessary to only reward themselves if their tasks were finished on time. But, we usually find that if a person begins skipping tasks or finishing tasks later than he had planned, he tends to return to less effective study techniques, like cramming before exams.

DEVELOPING A GRAPH

Important Steps in Developing a Graph

How can I use a graph to record my progress?
A graph is a good means of showing the achievement of tasks, which are counted as you complete them. Beverly, for example, might graph the number of questions and answers she has generated from text chapters, lecture notes, old tests, and so on.

When using a graph to record progress, how do I determine whether or not I've reached my goal?
Beverly's goal was to pass her test. She knew that, if she predicted and answered questions, she was likely to pass it. She asked herself, "How many questions and answers should I generate from lecture notes, chapters, and other sources to insure that I comprehend the material and pass the test?"

If she had developed 15 questions for each chapter and 6 for each lecture, she would have had 147 questions and answers at the end of 4 weeks. She would have distributed her work as follows:

Week	Chapters	Lectures	Total Questions
1	1, 2	1-3	48
2	3	4-6	33
3	4	7-9	33
4	5	10-12	33
			147

In making her graph, Beverly would put the number of tasks she had to accomplish on the vertical line. On the bottom, or horizontal, line she would list the amount of time she had to accomplish her tasks. The graph would look like this:

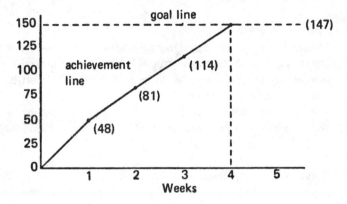

Achievement and Goal Lines

Beverly's goal line is drawn in the figure above. It shows her four-week goal: 147 questions and answers. Had she achieved her goal before four weeks were up, she would have crossed the goal line and continued to develop questions and answers. Most important, she would have known that she had accomplished her goal.

The achievement line is drawn to show the rate at which Beverly had to accomplish her tasks if she wished to reach her goal in four weeks. As she recorded her progress, she would see whether she was ahead of, keeping up with, or behind schedule. If she were behind, she would know it was time to get moving. If she were ahead of or on schedule, she could relax and turn to other activities.

Note: The tasks that you must accomplish (number of questions and answers, problems solved, pages read, pages written, and so on) are always listed along the vertical line. The amount of time you have in which to complete the tasks is always written across the bottom line.

Benefits of Graphing

How will the graph help Beverly to reach her goal of passing the test?
The graph will tell her how well she is predicting and answering questions that are likely to be on her test. She'll know how much time she has to complete her tasks and how many should be completed each week. She'll know whether she is ahead of or behind schedule. The achievement line serves this purpose. She'll be able to record her progress as soon as she completes each task. Finally and most important, though often overlooked, is that the graph will encourage her to reward herself for working to meet her goal.

REWARDING YOUR PROGRESS

The Importance of Rewards

Why is rewarding myself so important?
Most students try to escape from or avoid aversive situations. Students want to take the pressure off themselves, finish reading the stupid book, get the test over with, and keep from flunking out or doing poorly. In our estimation, this attitude is tragic. Students should enjoy going to school.

We have shown you a series of study skills that will make studying more enjoyable. We would like to increase your enjoyment of studying and doing well in school by encouraging you to reward yourself for accomplishing tasks and achieving goals.

Students often say: "Well, isn't rewarding myself bribery? Why should I reward myself for something I have to do?" The answer is simple: You're more likely to do what's good for you when you encourage yourself to do it. We suggest rewarding yourself with free time, television time, reading magazines, or whatever you enjoy. The rewards need not cost anything. Rewards may simply be opportunities to engage in activities that you enjoy. Go ahead and give yourself periodic rewards for accomplishing tasks.

Guidelines for the Use of Graphs, Checklists, and Rewards

Okay, I'll give the graph and checklist a try. Are there any special rules I should follow in using them?
Yes. We'd suggest, first, that you always *post* your graphs or checklists where they will be highly visible. Your checklists and graphs will serve as constant reminders of what you should be doing and how well you are doing it.

Second, ask yourself what you should really be able to do in the amount of time you have to accomplish your goal. *Schedule* your work, as we suggested earlier, so that all the work for a particular course isn't crammed into a short period of time. Spread your work out! Give yourself time to relax before the test or the date your paper is due.

Third, list the rewards that you will receive for accomplishing your goals. Always reward yourself as you accomplish your goals! Never cheat yourself!

The response from our students throughout the years to using checklists, schedules, and graphs has been exceedingly favorable. Students have enjoyed the benefits of having more predictable study schedules. Needless to say, students also enjoyed their rewards. Equally important, students have seen improvements in their grades. If you'd like the same results, we encourage you to give these tactics a try.

ACTION REVIEW:
CHECKLIST FOR SUCCESS IN SETTING
AND ACHIEVING STUDY GOALS

Y* N NI

1. ___ ___ ___ Do I set specific study goals for each course?
2. ___ ___ ___ Do I set up a schedule to achieve study goals?
3. ___ ___ ___ Do I record my progress at achieving study goals?
4. ___ ___ ___ When I achieve study goals, do I reward myself?

*Y = Yes
 N = No
 NI = Needs Improvement

CHAPTER 7

ERRONEOUS beliefs about instructors and Matching learning and teaching styles

DO YOU MAKE ERRONEOUS ASSUMPTIONS ABOUT YOUR INSTRUCTORS?

When you accept complete responsibility for learning as much as possible from your instructors, you're on the right track. You will get more than your money's worth from school. If, however, you assume that your instructors are responsible for your learning everything you want to know, you may become disappointed with your schooling.

A candid appraisal of instructors and of your assumptions about instructors will help you understand why many of your assumptions are not justified. When we teach, we sometimes ask students to list their assumptions and expectations about instructors. Then we compare the assumptions and expectations with reality. In the pages that follow, you will be able to discover which of your beliefs and expectations about instructors are erroneous and which are realistic.

In front of each statement you'll find two spaces. Check off whether or not you believe the statement.

We want you to learn about myths* which may be affecting your assumptions of what your instructors should be like. Most important, we want to encourage you to stop letting erroneous beliefs set you up to feel angry, disappointed, and discouraged.

After you have read through the myths, we'll talk about predictable conflicts between teaching styles and learning styles, some successful ways to gain as much as possible from a variety of different types of instructors, and what to avoid doing to alienate your instructors.

MYTHS ABOUT INSTRUCTORS

Yes	No		
—	—	Myth No. 1	Most college instructors are trained in how to be effective instructors.
		Reality:	Colleges usually assume that a person with a graduate degree in a subject should be able to teach it. Yet, few of your college instructors have received formal training in how to be effective teachers. New instructors learn how to teach through trial and error during their early years as instructors and assistant professors. Very few instructors receive training for one of their major responsibilities—TEACHING!

*As used in the chapter, the term "myth" means "A collective opinion, belief, or ideal that is based on false premises or is the product of fallacious reasoning." (Funk & Wagnalls' *Encyclopedic College Dictionary*)

Yes   No

—   —   Myth No. 2   All of your instructors will be interesting lecturers and devote considerable effort to making the course stimulating and motivating.

Reality: Most of your college instructors would like to be interesting, stimulating, and motivating lecturers. But, you will find that your instructors vary widely in their ability to maintain your interest. Some of your instructors will be downright boring and uninteresting regardless of how hard they try to maintain your interest. These instructors may still be excellent at presenting the information you want to learn. They are just not entertainers.

—   —   Myth No. 3   Your instructors will always be well prepared for each class you attend.

Reality: Most of your instructors will be well prepared for each class. Regardless of how well your instructors plan, sometimes a class won't work out as well as they hope. Some times, instructors' commitments and personal lives get in the way of their planning. They may come to class poorly prepared. Some of your instructors may even get to the point where they feel too confident and do little or no planning.

—   —   Myth No. 4   Every instructor will take a personal interest in you.

Reality: Some of your instructors will enjoy being more than just your instructor. These instructors will enjoy spending time conversing with you in class, abound campus, and socially in the community. But some of your instructors who are very popular because of excellent teaching, professional accomplishments, or just being nice people will face unrealistic demands from students. Popular instructors often do not have time to be all things to all people. Student and professional demands will often become stressful and create personal problems for popular instructors. Other instructors will simply not wish to do anything but teach and attend to their professional and personal lives. These very private individuals will often politely but firmly push student demands aside.

—   —   Myth No. 5   Your instructors want all ideas challenged and want students to present their opinions and views during class.

74

Yes   No

Reality: Many of your instructors will seek as much appropriate and useful student input as possible. A small proportion of your instructors will have little or no interest in students' opinions and views. Other instructors will feel that they have limited time to present vast amounts of important information. These instructors are often rather dedicated individuals who don't wish to offend students but very often discourage student input so as to maintain their schedule. For them, getting through the course material is more important than letting students express views.

— — Myth No. 6   Instructors want you to obediently accept everything they say without reservation and be able to accurately regurgitate on exams the truths they've taught.

Reality: Most instructors have two goals. One is for you to understand the basic facts and concepts in the field or subject being taught. The other is for you to learn to think for yourself. Once you gain a sense of these two goals you can learn the content of the course and at the same time question basic assumptions.

— — Myth No. 7   Your instructors will be pleasant people.

Reality: Many of your instructors will be people who have entered the teaching profession because they enjoy having a positive effect on other people. These instructors will often be pleasant to be around and have a profound effect on their students. A small proportion of your instructors will be neither pleasant nor unpleasant. These instructors will simply be there to help you learn. A very small proportion of your instructors will be irritable, unpleasant, and bores to be around. If you are asking the question, "Do I like this instructor?" you are asking the wrong question. The right question is, "Does this teacher know the subject well enough to teach me something?"

— — Myth No. 8   Your instructors will be able to answer all of your questions about the subject.

Reality: Most instructors see education as an ongoing process for themselves as well as for their students. Being well educated includes learning what you don't know. Being well educated is to discover

Yes   No

Reality: that some answers are partially true or only correct in certain circumstances.

Would you rather have an instructor who can give you what seems to be a definite, correct answer about everything or one who says, once in a while, "I don't know," and then suggests a way to find the answer?

One of the eventual results when you ask good questions and learn what the answers are is that you eventually run out of people who can answer your questions. Questions which no one can answer well are the forerunners of new knowledge, scientific advances, and exciting career directions.

—   —   Myth No. 9   Your instructors will know more than you.

Reality: If you've had a thirst for knowledge for many years, read a lot, and learned from life's experiences, you may find that you know more about some things than the instructor. As disappointing as this may be to you, the fact is that you may be too advanced for the class. If so, is that a legitimate excuse for being angry at the instructor or the school?

One of the signs of having an educated heart as well as an educated mind is that you can handle those times when you discover that someone with an advanced degree knows less about a topic than you. And if you think you understand the topic so well, how about taking your turn as a teacher? Are you ready for that?

—   —   Myth No. 10   Your instructor must have first-hand experience to be able to teach a subject well.

Reality: In trade schools, experience is essential. There are many courses, however, where the sniping comments such as "How can he know, he's never been there," only serve as a rationalization not to listen. An instructor in management can teach many practical ideas without ever having owned or run a business. A person can teach child development well without having had children. A psychologist can teach about mental disturbances without having been a mental patient. History and geography teachers can teach well without having "been there."

First-hand experience is very useful, but not

76

Reality: essential. In fact, many people with experience
don't know how to teach what they do. Have you
ever tried to learn from Granny exactly how she
makes that special dessert all the family loves? Or
ask Uncle Ned exactly how he knows which wood
to use? Asking "has the instructor had first-hand
experience" is asking the wrong question. Asking,
"can this instructor teach well" is the right
question.

YOUR ATTITUDES AFFECT YOUR SUCCESS IN SCHOOL

When we talk to students about the myths versus the realities of college instructors, we hear hilarious, empassioned, and periodically bitter stories of students' feelings for and against instructors. There is no question that your instructors' personalities and teaching behaviors will have a profound impact on your attitude toward learning and your performance in college. *What does all this mean for you?*

The reality of going to college is that you'll attend courses taught by instructors with just about every personality characteristic imaginable. You'll attend courses taught by highly competent instructors and less well-equipped instructors. That is simply the way things work.

What is important for you is that, YOU CAN MAKE YOUR ATTITUDES ABOUT INSTRUCTORS WORK FOR YOU OR AGAINST YOU! YOU CAN ATTEMPT TO GET THE MOST POSSIBLE OUT OF EVERY COURSE REGARDLESS OF YOUR INSTRUCTORS' PERSONALITIES OR LEVELS OF COMPETENCY. OR, YOU CAN GO AROUND COMPLAINING AND MOANING ABOUT WHY SOME OF YOUR INSTRUCTORS STINK AND WHY YOU ARE NOT LEARNING ANYTHING! IT IS ALL UP TO YOU!

PREDICTABLE CONFLICTS BETWEEN TEACHING AND LEARNING STYLES

Research into teaching effectiveness led psychologists to the questions: "Why do some students do well with one instructor but not another?" "Why do instructors do well with some students but not with others?"

Efforts to answer these questions uncovered a simple but relevant factor. It is that *the way some people teach doesn't always match up with the way other people learn.*

Based on the research and on our own experiences, here are some differences between students and instructors which lead to some predictable conflicts:

Auditory versus Visual Styles

Some people learn best by listening. Information doesn't stick well unless they hear it. Other people learn best by reading. They must see something before they believe it and remember it.

What is your natural preference?

Do you remember best what is said to you or what you read?

Do you prefer television or newspapers as your source of news?

Would you rather hear an expert talk on a subject or read what the expert has written?

If you have some spare time, would you rather sit around talking with people or go to the library and read?

If someone sends you a note setting up a time to get together, does the date really register with you or must you also hear them *say* to you when they will meet you?

If you are working with a group of people and there is some discrepancy between the written guidelines and the verbal instructions, which do you tend to believe?

Was reading the college catalog your main way of learning about your program and classes or did you merely skim the catalog and go see an advisor who told you everything you needed to know?

Everyone learns both ways, of course. We are not talking about an either/or situation. Yet, the differences between people are sometimes extreme enough to cause some basic problems. If you have a visual learning style, you operate mainly on the basis of what you read. You may have some difficulty with a verbal-auditory instructor who believes that merely telling people what to learn and know is sufficient.

If you have a verbal-auditory style, you will probably do well with an instructor who says everything to learn and do. You may have some difficulty with a visually oriented instructor who hands out a written statement about what to do to pass the course and who doesn't want to discuss it—who assigns textbook material and outside readings which are never discussed in class.

The solution, if you have an auditory orientation and are in a class taught by a visually oriented person is

1. Find classmates who will tell you what they learned from the textbook readings.
2. Dictate the main points from the reading assignments and handouts onto cassette tape and then listen to the tapes.
3. Consciously work at improving your ability to acquire information visually. For professional help, go to the reading improvement center.

If you learn best visually, then you may be in trouble with an instructor who doesn't use handouts or doesn't write much on the blackboard. You may have problems with instructors who use class discussion as a teaching tool.

The solution if you have a visual orientation in a class taught by a verbal-auditory instructor is

1. Take very good notes on what the instructor and your classmates say. After class fill in sentences and compare notes with other students.
2. Ask the instructor for suggested articles or books which cover the points you need to understand better.
3. Consciously work at listening and remembering what people say. *TIP:* Every so often, repeat back to the instructor what you believe has been said, for example, "Excuse me, I want to make sure I've accurately heard the main points. The main arguments in favor of the view are (_____); is that correct?"

Pedantic versus Metaphoric

Increased knowledge about the functions of the brain have changed the old views about how your brain operates. Years ago, students learned that their brains (the cerebral cortex) had two halves. These were referred to as the two hemispheres of the brain and one of the hemispheres was understood to be dominant over the other.

The newer view is that instead of conceptualizing what is inside your skull as a brain with halves, it is more accurate to think of yourself as having two brains. The *left* brain is where your speech center develops. Speech development is closely related to "handedness." With some exceptions, if you are right-handed your speech centers develop in your left brain. Once this occurs, many related functions develop in the left brain. Here is where you remember words, use logic, and think analytically and objectively about the world. The left brain makes possible your ability to think rationally and unemotionally. The left brain thinks in a linear fashion, following a logical sequence to an end point. It is time oriented.

The right brain carries your memory for music. You think visually, emotionally, and irrationally in the right brain. It is the source of creativity and intuition. Right brain thinking follows emotional logic. Using it, you can visualize and think in patterns jumping from one spot in a pattern to another without apparent logic or reason. Although it has no speech centers, a few words can come when going along with strong emotions or music. Stroke patients who have lost their powers of speech can, when upset, still swear. They can, when remembering a childhood melody such as "Twinkle, Twinkle Little Star," recall a few of the words. The right brain is your metaphoric mind. It focuses on the pattern and emotional truth of things with images which are like what is being experienced. For example, a woman trying to tell her group what it was like to live with her husband said, "With him what I get is like a long drought with an occasional thunderstorm; what I need is a gentle rain." Telling a child he "eats like is a pig" is a metaphoric statement.

If you tend to be a left brain person, then you will be well matched to an instructor who gives you a thorough, unemotional listing of facts, data, analytic explorations, hypotheses, logic, evidence, numbers, definition of terms, and rational conclusions.

If you tend to be left brained and get an instructor who teaches in a right-brained way, you may find the course to be a bewildering experience. You may have experienced the instructor as weird, too emotional, and a bit nutty. After all, there must be something wrong with a management instructor who reads poetry in class. And isn't it amazing how some students really enjoy it? They actually believe this is a great teacher and a wonderful class.

If you tend to be right brained with a left-brained teacher, the course will be painful for you. You'll feel like a thirsty person reaching for a glass of water only to discover that it is filled with sand. Something in you will be crying out, "Where is the heart? Why is there no life to this?" You may wonder, "Where is the humor, the drama, the excitement? These facts all seem to make sense, but what can I do with them? Why are we painstakingly dissecting every tree and plant when I want to experience the rich sweep of the forest?"

The solution to this sort of conflict, as we've stated before, is to *avoid indulging in the attitude, "If only other people would change, my world would be a better place for me."* You can try to find someone (perhaps even the instructor) who can translate the material presented to you in a form which you can understand better. More importantly, however we recommend that you work at gaining more use of your other brain.

The situation may not be easy at first, but it does give you a chance to add another dimension to yourself. And isn't that what you're in school for? *Remember: You do not have to give up your more natural and preferred way of thinking, feeling, and talking.* What you can do is add more to what you already have. We'll get into more of this in the chapter on the Survivor Personality. In that chapter, we've described the qualities of people who use both brains and show what advantages you gain.

Friendly versus Distant

Imagine your instructor stopping you as you leave the classroom and saying, "I liked the paper you turned in last week and want to talk with you about it. Do you have time to come and have a cup of coffee with me?"

How would you react? Would you be pleased and eagerly accept the invitation? Or would you draw back and make up an excuse to get away?

Just as it has been throughout your life, instructors and students vary considerably in regard to how friendly they want to be and how much distance they need to have. A friendly, extroverted instructor enjoys after-class contact with students. He or she will ask students to coffee, to evenings at the pizza house to talk and drink, and perhaps even to parties where the instructor lives. If you are similarly friendly and enjoy that, then you are going to have a wonderful year.

If you are a more introverted person, however, you may suffer a bit from personal attention and closeness. You would much rather have a quiet, tactful instructor who respects your need to be left alone. Such an instructor understands how embarrassing it is to be called on to talk in class or to be openly praised for getting a high score on an exam.

On the other hand, if you are a basically friendly person with a more introverted instructor, you may find it puzzling to have him or her pulling away from you after class. After all, what are instructors for if not to be available for students? Yet your inclination to want to be friendly and chat awhile may cause the instructor to stare at you and make an excuse to get away quickly. Then after that, you get the feeling that you are being avoided.

The solution that we recommend was covered earlier in this chapter. If an instructor doesn't live up to your expectations about what an instructor should be like, then question your "shoulds." When reality is inconsistent with your beliefs and erroneous expectations, then what is the best solution?

"External" versus "Internal" Learning Styles*

Some "external" learners are only open to believe information that comes from an authority or expert. Information or suggestions from other sources can't be trusted as accurate. If you prefer to get the guidance from expert sources and your instructor enjoys being an expert, then you have a good match.

The more you need an instructor who tells the class exactly what to learn, and then tests the class on how well they've done as told, then the better you will do with this type of instructor. If you need clear guidelines from instructors but take a course from someone who gives little clear direction, you may flounder awhile. You may be sitting in class waiting for the instructor to tell you what the answer to a problem is, only to have him or her ask the class, "What do you think?" And after waiting for the class to get through talking, the instructor may refuse to say what the right answer is. He or she may say, "You may be right," or, "There is some truth to that."

Some students react negatively to classes where the instructor encourages discussion and encourages students to develop their own views and answers. Their students protest, "I didn't pay good money to sit and listen to a bunch of uninformed people express their opinions. I can get that in any bar." This attitude is legitimate. It is also narrow minded.

The word *education* means to "draw out of." It does not mean "shovel into." A good education teaches you to think for yourself. It teaches you to ask good questions and then learn how to find the answers on your own. A good education does not give you a diploma for learning how to seek out an expert for any question you have. It teaches you how to both listen to authorities and come to your own conclusions.

The more you look to experts of a field of knowledge as providing you with "truth" and "reality," the more vulnerable you are to being misled by people who

Adapted from Julian Rotter in "Generalized Expectancies for Internal versus External Control of Reinforcement," *Psychological Monographs,* vol. 80, no. 1, 1966 and Herbert M. Lefcourt, *Locus of Control* (New York: Wiley, 1976).

need to be admired as experts. The more that you find a workable balance between objective facts, your own knowledge, and good judgment, the more you will develop internally guided direction in your life.

"Internal" learners who have a clear sense of self direction need and appreciate an instructor who will let them follow their own path. Such students get upset with instructors who tell them exactly what they must learn, in what way, and how they will demonstrate what they have learned. For them, a clearly defined course structure is abrasive. They feel handicapped more than helped. Such reactions are legitimate and narrow minded.

In every field of study, certain basics must be mastered. There are basic terms and concepts which must be understood. There are some techniques which are fundamental to mastery of the subject even though the reasons why may not be given, or when given don't make sense.

Being Both "Internal" and "External" in Learning

Our experience is that the students who get the most out of school can discipline themselves to follow the tightly controlled steps used by some teachers and create their own learning experiences when in a class taught by someone who gives few guidelines. (See the attitude survey on pp. 103-104.)

If you find yourself in a class where the instructor is overly controlling or overly permissive then:

1. Ask for what you want. Ask the permissive instructor for more structure if you need that. Ask the controlling instructor for freedom to do something different if you want that. You may be surprised at how easy it is to get what you want when you ask.
2. If asking doesn't work—or you don't want to ask—then try to adapt to your instructor's style. Instead of being angry at what the world has served up, see what you can learn from doing it the instructor's way. You may be surprised at what you discover.

Curve Grading versus Contracts

Viewing the instructor as an authority who tells you what to learn is usually linked to expecting the instructor to decide what grade you will receive. The traditional method of teaching usually implies using a class curve to determine student grades.

Grading "on the curve" means that all the scores are ranked from highest to lowest. Then the few highest scores are given "As." The next group, down to the midpoint in the class, receive "Bs." Students whose scores fall below the class midpoint receive "Cs". Any students with scores below a certain minimum level receive "Ds" and "Fs."

Smart, hard-working, competitive students tend to like curve grading. Their "As" indicate that they are better than most other students. The problem with curve grading is that students who are not competitive may not even try. Curve grading increases competitiveness between students and decreases cooperation.

Students are less likely to share notes, join together in study groups, or help each other because helping the other person may give them a higher score and thus lower your grade. With curve grading, only a limited number of "As" and "Bs" are available.

Curve grading increases stresses and tensions when all the students in a certain class are good students. In such a class, anyone under the midpoint will get a "C" even though the same examination score in another class might be up in the "B" group.

To encourage good students to take courses where they might not do better than average, many colleges offered a new option. Some courses could be taken on a pass/no pass basis. With this option, a student can take a class which will broaden his or her education and earn credit for the course without a grade being assigned. Students taking pass/no pass courses can earn credit toward graduation requirements without risking lowering their Grade Point Average (G.P.A.).

To reduce competition and yet encourage good work, many instructors now teach their courses using a "contract" approach. The contract is that the instructor agrees at the beginning of the course to give you whatever grade you want to earn by doing a specific amount of work with a specific quality. You decide at the beginning what you grade you want to receive in this class. Earning an "A", "B", or "C" is completely your choice.

The instructor has decided before the start of the course what activities and demonstrations of learning are worth an "A", what you must do to earn a "B", and what a "C" is worth. Then the instructor makes an agreement with you—that is, enters into a "contract" with you—guaranteeing that for doing the work you will get the grade you want.

This contract method may seem strange to you if you are expecting the old "grading on the curve" method. Some students are bewildered when they first encounter it. They are not used to the freedom and the responsibility. If you are not used to this approach, don't let it throw you. Once you get used to it, you'll probably like it better than the old way. With the contract approach, you will find that you don't have to compete with anyone except yourself. If you get a low grade, however, you are stuck with the knowledge that it was your own fault. You can't blame the other students for beating you out. You can't blame the instructor for being arbitrary or unclear.

The standards for "A" grades are usually high, but in the class working together to learn, there may be 50 to 70 percent of the class earning "As". Who knows, with this sort of an opportunity you may do much better in school than you expect. You may become one of the many students who qualify for membership in Phi Beta Kappa, the national scholastic honorary society.

Three Basic Teaching Styles

STUDENT CENTERED

The contract method of determining grades is well suited to the instructor who makes students the focus of attention in the course. The instructor's main concern

83

is your progress and development. Your personal growth is more important than the college, the instructor, the subject matter, or the discipline.

The instructor sees his or her primary responsibility as one of teaching students, not English, math, or chemistry. Such an instructor may be described as *altruistic*. The approach is a selfless enjoyment in the experience of students gaining knowledge and understanding. Time outside the classroom is devoted more to grading class work and conferring with students than in doing the research and publishing that the college wants.

Several disadvantages to having an instructor who teaches in a student centered fashion are

You may have to do more work. The instructor wants papers, projects, and reports as a way of monitoring your progress.

You will be more than a face in the crowd. Your level of understanding, your study habits, and your ways of thinking may be seen for what they are. Some students can't handle that.

The instructor may make outrageous statements, challenge viewpoints, or take shocking positions in the service of getting you to think. This might not be a pleasant process if you dislike disagreement and conflict.

The instructor may give students little to imitate. Instead of giving students a model to follow or a clear way of thinking and acting that can be imitated, this instructor works at developing individuality. The goal is for everyone to discover their individual abilities and natures rather than to become like the instructor.

SUBJECT CENTERED

Some instructors make the subject matter of the course the main focus of attention. The more you share the instructor's awe, respect, and enthusiasm for the subject, the better you will do. With such an instructor, be prepared for an endless parade of glimpses at this field of study which he or she finds so absorbing.

In contrast to the student centered approach, this instructor may be irritated with students who reject or challenge the views presented. Much preferred are brief sharings or insights and any supporting evidence you have found.

For some students, the instructor is a model to imitate. They adopt the instructor's vocabulary, clothing, and views.

Some disadvantages are

In its extreme, the content centered instructor is a sort of recruiter. He or she wants to draw students into a professional career in this field.

The instructor gains power over the student by becoming a coach on how to make it all the way through to the inside.

The student must adopt a certain viewpoint and vocabulary which may reduce and limit self-development.

INSTRUCTOR CENTERED

Every campus has instructors who sparkle with charisma. They are exciting, inspired teachers. They can capture a room full of students and hold a class spellbound with extraordinary stories, histrionics, and impassioned appeals. They command attention. Their field of expertise as a medium, the classroom is their stage.

In such classes, your efforts to speak up or share your own experiences may not be well received. The charismatic instructor tends to be impatient when others become the center of attention. The purpose of the lecture hour is to inspire and motivate, not for students to discuss or share.

If you enjoy good performances and welcome inspirational lectures, you are well matched. If, on the other hand, you would rather have many pages of notes full of information at the end of the lecture, you may be disappointed.

Some disadvantages with charismatic, instructor centered classes are:

Your questions will be reacted to, but not usually well answered because the instructor will be playing to the audience.

To be in the spotlight, the instructor may use the classroom as a forum to attack his or her profession and colleagues. Instead of learning about the value of the subject, you may learn what is wrong with it.

Although you are absorbed and captivated during lectures, you may realize later that you haven't learned many facts. You may find that most of your factual learning comes from the textbook and that the instructor gives the text little attention in class.

IDEAL

The best all-around teachers are usually some combination of all of the above. The more capable teachers enjoy having a room full of students eager to listen and learn. They enjoy being appreciated for their teaching skills. Good teachers like the subject and value their chosen field. They encourage student growth and make themselves available for conferences and discussions.

REALITY

What do you do when a teacher is less than ideal? Do you get angry when you discover that you don't have a good match between yourself and the instructor?

What can you do if the instructor doesn't seem to know how to quiet several talkative students? Can you still learn something from an instructor whose religious or political views are contrary to yours? And what if you hear gossip that the instructor uses marijuana or has had an affair with a student?

By now we hope that you begin to realize, if you didn't know already, that finding a really good match between yourself and an instructor is not something that happens all the time. If one of your habits is to find something wrong with others, your instructors will give you plenty of opportunities. If you are an experienced "victim," then the college will provide you with many chances to be upset, complain to classmates, and attack instructors you've judged to be imperfect.

Additional Suggestions

As an alternative to being a "victim," we have these suggestions:

Ask around before registration to find out who the more well regarded instructors are. If you have a choice between instructors, you'll know which one to choose.

When you have a problem getting in touch with what is happening in a course, make an appointment to talk with the instructor. Be prepared to ask for what you want.

Try to get as much out of every course regardless of who your instructor is or how much the teaching style does not fit your preferred learning style. Be open to try a new way of learning.

If you still have problems, go to the office or center which teaches studying and reading skills. The counselors there can be very helpful.

Most important, be active in helping your instructors become better instructors.

CHAPTER 8

HOW TO iNFLUENCE YOUR iNSTRUCTORS

© 1972 United Feature Syndicate, Inc.

HELPING YOUR INSTRUCTORS BE BETTER INSTRUCTORS

If you say to yourself, *"It's my job to help my instructors do well!"* you can have a profound effect on your instructors' performance. There are many things you can do as a student to make the lives of your instructors more pleasant and their performance more useful to you. Here is what students who get better teaching suggest.

Reward Your Instructors for Good Teaching

When your instructors do something that you consider to be effective teaching, let your instructors know that you appreciate their teaching. Rewards for good teaching are few and far between. After a better than average lecture, tell your instructor in a few well-thought-out words what you liked about the lecture. Most students are reluctant to compliment their instructors. Most students don't want to appear to be apple polishers. Your instructors will probably be excellent judges of sincere comments and will appreciate what you have to say. Don't hold back your compliments. Let your instructors know you like their teaching.

Know What You Want and Have a Positive Action Plan

Do you know exactly what things instructors do that make them good instructors? Can you clearly describe the specific, observable behaviors that you know are the basis for good teaching?

Action Project

Step 1   TAKE A FEW MINUTES TO LIST ALL THOSE THINGS THAT GOOD TEACHERS DO. LIST SPECIFICS. LIST OBSERVABLE BEHAVIORS. (For example: "Listens attentively when I ask a question." *NOT* "is nice.")

Get together with several other students and compare lists. Discuss the lists and revise them.

Step 2   BRAINSTORM A LIST OF ALL THE REINFORCING THINGS YOU COULD DO IN RESPONSE TO A DESIRED TEACHING BEHAVIOR

To brainstorm means to write out a list of ideas as fast as you can. The emphasis is on quantity, not quality. Be wild and imaginative. Be outrageous and funny. Do this with three or four other people and see how much fun brainstorming can be.

After about five minutes, stop and go through the list to see what things you could do. *Note:* You will continue to come up with ideas for the list for a few more hours, so wait a day or so before finishing your basic list.

Step 3   TYPE OUT A COPY OF YOUR LISTS OF DESIRED TEACHING BEHAVIORS AND TEACHER REINFORCERS AND PLACE IT IN YOUR NOTEBOOK.

Step 4   NOW LOOK FOR THE FIRST POSSIBLE OPPORTUNITY TO OBSERVE A GOOD TEACHING BEHAVIOR AND REWARD IT!

Pay Attention to Your Instructors

Pay close attention to what your instructors say in class. If you don't see why your attention is important, imagine standing in front of a group of students who are nodding off to sleep, gazing out windows, carrying on private conversations, and generally acting disinterested. Would you be motivated to be enthusiastic and well prepared to teach this group of students?

Encourage Good Instructional Behavior

When your instructors are doing things which you consider to be good teaching, be very attentive. Nod; even smile. Instructors' actions are determined to a large extent by the attention they receive from students. When you and the other students indicate your approval for your instructors' good teaching behavior, you'll encourage your instructors to do more of the things you like and less of what you don't like.

If you have any doubt about the effect sincere appreciation has on instructors think about your own experiences. Think about the motivating effects that compliments have had on you.

Provide Your Instructors with Feedback

If your Instructors encourage periodic evaluations of their classroom performance, be sure to fill out their evaluations. Let your instructors know what you like! If you want to tell an instructor that there is something which needs to be improved, be sure to give an example of what you don't like and what you would like. There are few things worse than having a student tell you to improve some aspect of your teaching behavior, but not be able to give you a clear example of what it is the student would like you to do. Be sure you can give an example of what you would like to see more or less of (for example, clearer instructions and fewer personal stories).

Help Your Instructor Be Clear and Precise

Encourage your instructors to clearly define their expectations of students. If your instructor is unclear as to an assignment, pleasantly ask him to restate the assignment. Don't hesitate to ask for clarification. If you didn't understand the assignment, more than likely other more timid students are sitting in class saying to themselves, "What is it he wants us to do?" You'll be doing yourself, your fellow students, and your instructor a favor by asking for a clarification.

Regardless of how unclear an instructor may be, when you ask your clarifying question, don't make a big deal about how confused you are. Don't make your instructor look like an idiot. Just ask your instructor to clarify what he wants and thank him for his help.

If after asking for clarification regarding an assignment you are still confused, don't badger the instructor. Try not to say things like, "I still don't know what you want!" or "You really haven't been clear as to the assignment!" More than likely, you and several other students can figure out what your instructor is assigning. If not, step up after class and pleasantly point out your confusion. When you ask for clarification, ask confidently, try not to play the "bewildered idiot."

Unclear questions from instructors often turn students' stomachs. You're likely to think to yourself, "What the hell is it he's asking?" Don't let your gut reaction show! Pleasantly ask your instructor to restate his question. Very often instructors don't think through their questions before asking students for answers. If you just say, "I am not sure I understood the question," you won't make your instructor look the fool. If your instructor takes a second to rephrase his question, both of you will be saved some anxiety. If your instructor's second attempt isn't any clearer than his first attempt, pleasantly indicate that you're unsure of the answer. Try to avoid throwing your hands into the air and saying, "I don't know what you're getting at!"

Prepare Good Questions Before Going to Class and Always Try to Answer Your Instructors' Questions

As you read your assignments for class, decide what questions you would like your instructor to answer. In class, listen attentively to see if your instructor answers your questions. If not, don't be reluctant to pose your questions to your instructor.

Most instructors want students to ask good questions. Too often, students sit back timidly, afraid to ask questions. Instructors then go into a sweat worrying whether or not the students have the least idea of what's going on.

Instructors prepare lectures hoping to stimulate students' inquisitiveness. If you sit back and fail to ask questions or turn your face to the floor every time an instructor poses a question, both your and the instructor will be losers. Give your instructors opportunities to demonstrate their intelligence. Ask good questions! Give yourself an opportunity to demonstrate your intelligence. Answer your instructors questions!

Attend All Classes

Instructors work hard to prepare lectures. When you decide to skip a class, you are saying to your instructors, "I don't believe what you are doing is of any value!" Show your instructors by your attendance that you value what they have to say.

Turn in Your Assignments on Time

Late assignments often suggest to your instructors that you lack enthusiasm for their courses. Some instructors reciprocate with a lack of enthusiasm for your procrastination by deducting points from late papers. Do your best to show you care. Don't say it with flowers! Say it with papers!

THE GRAND SCHEME: POSITIVE AND NEGATIVE EFFECTS

Students who get better teaching discover that POSITIVE STUDENT BEHAVIOR LEADS TO POSITIVE INSTRUCTOR BEHAVIOR.

Although our students have never claimed that reinforcing good teaching will turn an instructor from a "Simon Legree" into a "Dale Carnegie," students who actively work to get better teaching are emphatic about the positive effect students can have on instructor performance.

What are the negative by-products of student behavior?
Students who are aware of the effects students have on instructors are equally emphatic about the profound negative effect students can have on instructors' behavior.

NEGATIVE STUDENT BEHAVIOR CAN LEAD TO NEGATIVE INSTRUCTOR BEHAVIOR

Students are wonderful at describing ways to destroy the best of instructors. Some students gleefully describe stories relating how they spearheaded a well-planned attack on a high school teacher whom the students loathed. The sadistic glee of students is often shared by class members who remember a teacher from high school who found ill-prepared, unmotivated, and uncaring students too much to deal with.

Strangely enough, when college students somewhat shamefully list their adolescent behaviors, they often realize what a damaging effect their behavior may have had on that disliked high school instructor. Some high school teachers literally find the inconsiderate, unmotivated, and lackluster students not worth the effort. These unhappy instructors eventually resign themselves to collecting their paychecks and putting up with the daily task of teaching the "ungrateful."

The lot of the college instructor can sometimes be equally disheartening. College professors are known to complain of unmotivated, uncaring, and ill-prepared students. The cause of the professor's distress is often subtle and hopefully unconscious student behavior. In defense of themselves, college students often point out how unaware they are of the effect of their behavior on professors.

As is often the case, people are unaware of the effects of their behavior on others until it is too late. In your case, there has never been a better time to observe the behavior of college students which creates rather frustrated professors.

Notice Negative Effects on Your Instructors

As you go through the list of "Behaviors Guaranteed to Frustrate Instructors," ask yourself

How often have I behaved this way to an instructor?
What effect would this behavior have on me if I were the instructor?
If I were the instructor, how would I respond to students who acted in such ways?

By taking the perspective of your instructor, you may get a better feeling for why it's academic suicide to get caught up in behaving inconsiderately toward your instructors. You may appreciate how easily professors can become disheartened by nice students who simply aren't aware of what it's like to deal with well-meaning but unthinking students.

BEHAVIORS GUARANTEED TO FRUSTRATE INSTRUCTORS

Angry Arguments with Instructors, Especially over Exams

Students consistently describe instances in which frustrated classmates verbally attack instructors' statements. Sure, you have a right to your opinion. But, regardless of how seriously you differ with your instructor, you needn't argue. A huffy, heated attack on your instructor's position will gain neither of you anything but a mutual dislike for one another.

Useful alternative: Learn to present your difference of opinion assertively but without anger. Ask questions to find out why the differences exist. Turn the conflict into a learning experience.

Treat Classes as Social Hours or as Unwanted Obligations

For a variety of reasons, students often carry on private conversations, act bored, show up late, sleep, leave class early, or simply play the fool in class. You wouldn't be paid for sleeping, playing cards, or socializing with your best friend if you were working a nursing shift or acting as foreman on an assembly line. Instructors are justified to feel that you don't belong in their courses if you appear to be disinterested in learning.

Be a Know-it-all Student

We've all experienced the know-it-all students who act as though no one has anything to say of importance but them. Know-it-alls are universally hated! Our students have heard comments to know-it-alls such as, "Oh, we don't get to hear from you again do we?" or "You're so smart! You always have the final word!"

Useful alternative: If you treat other students as valuable people from whom you can learn, you'll be way ahead of the game. Assume that everyone has something to say of value. Acknowledge other students' contributions. If you spend time trying to prove that your instructors and fellow students know less than you, you can bet you'll come out on the short end of the stick.

Tell Emotional and Personal Stories Leading Nowhere

Students often become so involved with class discussions that they go off into personal stories which are of no value to anyone. Instructors are just as guilty of overpersonalizing their courses. There are times when our personal experiences are relevant to the focus of class discussion. We simply urge you to always ask yourself, "Will the personal comment I'm going to make add to the class discussion, or do I just want to tell people about myself?"

Periodically, the focus of a class discussion can lead people to become heated, angry, elated, joyous, or just about any emotional state imaginable. When you become emotional in class, if you're like most people, you may have a tendency to allow your mouth to run off with your emotions. Students often define such emotional behavior as "spilling your guts." We've all spilled our guts at times. We're all human. But, if you choose to avoid gut spilling, learn to ask yourself, "Do I really want to say what I am going to say when I feel like this? Do I want to think about what I am responding to and be sure that what I have to say is of value? If I do say something, need I be emotional?"

Useful alternative: Learning to think about what you're going to say and why you're going to say it is a skill everyone needs to practice. In your case, the crucial questions are, "Will what I say be of value?" and "How can I say what I want so as to ensure it will be most useful to other people?"

Expect Your Instructors to Be Outstanding Every Day

All of us have days when we'd prefer to avoid contact with other people. Professors do not have the luxury of hiding in a closet until a bad mood passes. If they haven't had time to prepare for class, they still have to show up.

Useful alternative: Show a little compassion. Don't expect the impossible. No one can be outstanding daily. If your professor appears to be having an off day, work your hardest to do everything possible to make the class a good one. Be more attentive than ever. Ask good questions. Nod and smile at everything your instructor does well. (A word of caution: Don't overdo it. You needn't look like a smiling Cheshire cat. Just be positive.)

After class, if you liked your instructor's performance, go out of your way to let him know he did well. It's doubly important on tough days for instructors to know that they can ride out a storm.

Tell Other Students What You Dislike About the Instructor—Never Go Directly to the Instructor

It is easy for you to complain to other students about a particular instructor. The problem is that your complaints won't help your instructor teach better or your classmates learn more. Your complaints may result in students responding negatively toward your instructor, which will surely hurt his performance. So why make things tough for your instructor, your fellow students, and yourself?

Useful alternative: Encourage other students to get the most out of your instructors' courses. Never downgrade your instructors to other students. Try to help your instructors, not hurt them! Encourage yourself and other students to look for the good points in your instructors. As we've stated throughout this chapter, try to create a climate in which your instructors can do an even better job.

If you decide that you just don't have the time or interest to help your instructors improve their performance, at least keep your negative comments to yourself. Don't make other students suffer who are willing to try to help your instructors.

Be Irritating to an Instructor Who Irritates You

Don't cut class, drop the course, or transfer to another class when you have a rotten instructor. Attend class and do things that communicate your negative opinion.

Take a paperback book to class and read it while the instructor lectures.

If you knit, take your knitting to class and work on it instead of taking notes. Click the needles loudly if you can.

Sit back with your arms crossed and refuse to take any notes while everyone else is writing furiously. Scowl and sneer at those who are taking notes.

Just as the instructor leads up to an important point in the lecture, lean over and whisper loudly to a classmate. Include muffled laughs and snickers. Keep it up, pretending not to notice how distracting your whispering is to the class and how angry the teacher is getting.

Talk Down to Instructors You Think Are "Losers"

If you have six or seven instructors you will probably feel that one of them is excellent, most of the others are adequate and that one is a loser. Here is a great opportunity to sneer at, be sarcastic with, and show open contempt for a teacher. You can prove to other students that you are so tough and "with it" you can put down instructors to their faces.

Useful Alternative: If you can't avoid being sarcastic then consider not saying anything at all. It is tough enough being an instructor. Especially when you know that some of the students openly dislike you. Instructors have all the fears that you might have if you had to make useful presentations to the same group day after day.

Remember too that it is a function of your human nature to like one of your instructors the best and another the least. If you really wanted better teaching you could give the instructor a sincere compliment after a better than average lecture. You could do the various things that preceded this section. If you are critical of teachers in a way that is not helpful or useful to them, you need to have a target for your disgust more than you need good teaching so don't take yourself too seriously!

Ask Your Instructors to Be Personal Counselors

It's natural for you to want to be friendly with your instructors. That's great! Unfortunately, some students expect too much of them. These students expect their instructors to be terribly interested in all of their personal ideas, interests, and problems. Most instructors want to be friendly with their students, but are not in a position to be all things to all students.

The difficulties begin to arise when students begin dropping in all the time to talk, unload about their personal problems, and generally cut into the rather tight schedules that many professors work within. Professors often feel uncomfortable discouraging drop ins. Few professors want to be known as uncaring or uninterested in their students. Professors want the best for their students and are usually willing to try to help. It's simply unfair to ask professors to spend their time socializing on the job or solving your personal problems.

Useful alternative: Try not to ask your instructors to do more than they are professionally equipped to handle. If you need help with personal problems, see the professional counselors at your college or talk to your best friends.

Demand that Your Instructors Give You Special Favors and Consideration

If you think we're making a big deal out of nothing, let that thought pass. We've known students who will miss half of the semester, come in, and ask if they can't somehow get the information from the instructor. We've known students who would ask instructors if they could take the mid-term two weeks late because they were leaving early on spring break for a vacation in Florida. Our favorite is the student who called an instructor at 8:00 a.m. on Saturday to find out if he missed anything important during the week of classes he missed.

Useful alternative: Most of your instructors will be people who are interested in your academic and personal well-being. Instructors understand that you may run into financial, transportation, health, and numerous problems which interfere with successful performance in class. Don't be afraid to let your instructor know when an event drastically alters your performance. If you're ill for two weeks with the flu, let your instructor know why you're missing class. Instructors appreciate knowing why students aren't coming to class.

Minor problems should be kept to yourself. If your car breaks down and you miss class, don't come in with a big song and dance expecting your instructor to pray for your car. Accept the bad with the good. Borrow notes from someone in the course. Don't expect your instructor to repeat an entire lecture for you.

In short, if something of tremendous importance necessitates you needing to ask a favor from your instructor, DON'T HOLD BACK!!!! If minor irritations of life have made your student life a bit miserable, assume you'll recover. Don't throw your personal problems at your instructor. What you'll probably find is that you'll live happily ever after.

"HOW CAN I TURN A BAD SITUATION AROUND?"

Avoid Flunking Courses by Being Diplomatic and Willing to Work

If you are likely to receive a "D" or "F" in a course, you can often salvage a bad grade. But, you have to learn to be diplomatic and pleasant to deal with.

Too often students having academic problems approach instructors with un-believable stories rather than accepting that a straightforward approach is best.

Go talk to your instructor and ask for a chance to make up your work. *Go with a plan!* Offer to make up exams. Ask if you can write an extra paper or rewrite the project you threw together the night before it was due. Explain why you are willing to. Instructors are much more willing to give students a chance to make amends if the students act like adults and are willing to admit that they have done poorly and are willing to turn over a new leaf rather quickly.

Most instructors will give you a chance. Bad grades are not permanent unless you allow them to be.

For example, if you do poorly on the mid-term or final, ask to take the make-up exam. Ask for a chance to show that you do know the material. (Maybe you didn't then but things have changed now.) Even if the instructor says you can't take the test to change your grade, ask to take it anyway to see for yourself if you can do better. Assuming that you will get a better score, this will have a psychological effect on the instructor later.

If you anticipate a bad grade in a course because you haven't been able to get all of the work in, and you want to earn a good grade, then consider asking the instructor to submit an "incomplete" on the grade sheet. Your instructor may be willing to follow school policies which allow students to complete course work after the course is over. At most schools you have at least a semester.

You can change the past if you want to. A sincere request for another chance, a specific plan about what you will do, and commitment to do it will influence the hardest of instructors and deans.

INSTRUCTORS ARE HUMAN BEINGS

The list of "Behaviors Guaranteed to Frustrate Instructors" is not meant to convey the message that instructors are special people who have to be treated with kid gloves. Absolutely not! Instructors are human beings who react just as you do to pressures, demands, problems, stresses, and all the other factors that complicate our lives.

Instructors are human beings just like you. They prefer to be treated nicely. They want you to come to their classes and learn every good thing you ever wanted to know. Most instructors will work overtime to help you. If you'll look for the good in your instructors and try to make their classes pleasant and enlightening, most of them will do everything humanly possible to make your life as a student a good life.

But remember, if you ask too much of your instructors, cut into their personal lives, appear disinterested in their courses, or generally make a pest of yourself, you'll encourage your professors to be sullen and angry individuals. You'll hear instructors who complain about not having enough time to get their work done. You'll hear professors griping about students who don't show up in class, don't ask good questions, don't seem to be interested in learning, and all in all are no joy to teach.

What we're suggesting to you is the simple fact that YOU MAKE A DIFFERENCE! YOU CAN EITHER CHOOSE TO HELP YOUR INSTRUCTORS BE BETTER INSTRUCTORS WHO ENJOY TEACHING OR YOU CAN CHOOSE TO BEHAVE IN WAYS WHICH CAUSE INSTRUCTORS TO BE UNHELPFUL AND BORING. INSTRUCTORS WHO GO AROUND WITH A CHIP ON THEIR SHOULDERS ARE OFTEN CREATED BY STUDENTS WHO DON'T APPEAR TO CARE ABOUT THEIR EDUCATION. The choice is yours. We suspect you'll want to do your best to help your instructors do their best possible for you and your fellow students.

Last but not least, accept the fact that you will have great instructors, mediocre instructors, and some who appear to be children of Satan. Regardless, follow the suggestions we've made. Try to help every instructor be a good instructor. It's all up to you!

ACTION PROJECT FOR GETTING BETTER TEACHING

1. _____ Take some time with several classmates to develop a list of things which good teachers do. List specific, observable behaviors.

2. _____ List all those things you might do that could be rewarding for an instructor.

3. _____ Observe each instructor to see how much or how little the desired teaching behaviors occur.

4. _____ Compliment and reward instructors who do many of the things you list as good teaching. Be specific. Let instructors know what you appreciate. *Remember:* The more quickly you reward a desired behavior, the more effective your reward.

5. _____ Observe how you react when a teacher is less than what you would like. Ask yourself, "Do I do any of the things which upset and frustrate teachers?"

6. _____ Track positives. When an instructor is low in giving you good

teaching behaviors, look for any little signs of improvement and immediately reinforce the improvement.

7. _____ Ask yourself, "Am I a rewarding person to have in class?" If you aren't, then here is a good chance to practice. *Remember:* Trite as it is, there is a lot of wisdom in the old idea of "An apple for the teacher!"

chapter 9

Learning habits
Review

© United Feature Syndicate, Inc.

Now that you have read and thought about ways to be more successful at learning, take a minute to review your progress. Use the following list to indicate what learning skills you presently have and those you'd like to have a year from now.

There's never been a more important time to evaluate yourself and decide upon a course of action.

Directions: On each of the folowing items, rate yourself as you are now and as you would like to be a year from now. Use these numbers:

(1) almost never
(2) sometimes
(3) half the time
(4) usually
(5) always

	Now	A Year from Now
1. Skim newly acquired course books to determine what important questions will be answered in the books.	___	___
2. Begin courses by asking instructors questions about course goals and requirements.	___	___
3. Attend classes.	___	___
4. Take good lecture notes.	___	___
5. Use a study schedule.	___	___
6. Minimize study distractions.	___	___
7. Consciously work at developing good study habits.	___	___
8. Study for short, realistic time spans.	___	___
9. Mix study subjects.	___	___
10. Study by asking and answering questions.	___	___
11. Make up and practice taking tests.	___	___
12. After studying for limited periods of time, relax and have fun.	___	___
13. Use all library resources well when writing papers.	___	___
14. Work at learning the most from each instructor.	___	___
15. Enjoy learning and being successful in courses.	___	___
16. Behave in positive ways to encourage good teaching.	___	___
17. Reward myself for reaching my goals.	___	___

On the other hand, if the foregoing is not for you, then here is a

CHECKLIST OF WAYS GUARANTEED TO UPSET RELATIVES, FRUSTRATE INSTRUCTORS, AND FORCE ADMINISTRATORS TO REVEAL THEIR TRUE CHARACTER BY PUTTING YOU ON ACADEMIC PROBATION

____ Study with the television turned on.

____ Avoid the library except to read magazines and check out the action.

____ Get into fights with my family and blame them for my difficulties.

____ Do not take notes in class.

____ Sit back and wait to see if the instructor can get my attention.

____ Find reasons and excuses for not doing what the instructor requests.

____ Daydream. Sit and stare out the window wishing I were someplace else.

____ Whisper and pass notes to other students.

____ Pretend I'm taking notes while writing a letter to someone.

____ Never ask questions in class.

____ Find something about the instructor that I don't like—posture, clothing, voice, way of lecturing, etc.

____ Gossip to other students about what upsets me but don't tell the instructor.

____ Wait until the last minute to do papers and copy the work of others.

____ Wait until the last minute to study, decide that it's too late to start now, and go to a movie instead.

____ Expect instructors to adapt their instruction to my learning style.

____ During exams sit near good students and copy their answers.

____ After doing all the above, blame the school for being such a crappy place, the instructors for being incompetent, and the administration for being _____ (fill in your own favorite term).

Do you recognize yourself in any of the above? This second list is to make you aware of habits you now have which lead to poor results in school. The point is that *everything you do has an effect on your success in college!* One set of habits leads to very little learning; the other set of habits leads to good learning. The choice is yours.

CHAPTER **10**

Characteristics of successful and unsuccessful students

© 1967 United Feature Syndicate, Inc.

Alice juggled her lunch tray and looked around the noisy cafeteria. She spotted Cheryl, her floor counselor, eating with several other students from the dorm. Alice walked over, and as she sat down, Cheryl asked the group, "Guess what is the most difficult problem for college students."

"Money!"

"Competition for grades."

"Not enough time."

"Parking?"

"Required courses."

"Schedule conflicts."

"Too many assignments."

Cheryl shook her head and said, "Wrong! The problem is too much freedom."

Alice asked, "Freedom?"

"Yes."

"During high school your work week was scheduled. Even study periods. You were told what to study. Even during study periods you were told what to study. Your life was structured by others. Now you don't have much structure. That's why so many students don't make it. Look at how many students wander around after class looking for something to happen. They've never had to oraganize their school lives."

Alice said, "Freedom to me means that I am now the one responsible for what I do, and I get to decide what I do! I love it!"

Cheryl said, "Good. I wish more students had that attitude. Unfortunately, they don't. So I get these lost souls who are looking for someone to tell them what to do. I wish there were an easy way to convince students that their attitudes about themselves and their lives determine how well their lives go for them."

Attitudes are mental and emotional habits. Like all habits, they are learned. Also, like other habits, they occur without conscious effort. Because they are learned, you can do something about counterproductive attitudes that work against you reaching your goals.

We find students in every class who are getting grades lower than they would like to have. They have a conscious desire to do better, but some unconscious atittudes work against it. Can you do anything about this problem? Yes. William James said the greatest discovery of his time is that by changing your attitudes, you can change your life.

The first step we have to take is to find out your attitude toward the idea that you can do anything about how things go for you. Take several minutes right now to do through the attitude survey which follows.

ATTITUDE SURVEY

From each pair of alternatives below, select the one that most closely represents your personal belief:

1. __ Promotions are earned through hard work and persistence. __ Promotions usually come from having the right people like you.

2. ___ How hard I study determines the grades I get.

___ I would get better grades if the teaching in this school were better.

3. ___ The increasing divorce rate indicates that fewer people are trying to make their marriages last.

___ Fate determines how long a marriage will last. All you can do is hope your partner will stay with you for life.

4. ___ When I want to, I can usually get others to see things my way.

___ It is useless to try to change another person's opinions or attitudes.

5. ___ In our society, a person's income is determined largely by ability.

___ Finding a well-paying job is a matter of being luckier than the next guy.

6. ___ If I handle people right, I can usually influence them.

___ I have very little ability to influence people.

7. ___ My grades are a result of my effort. Luck has little to do with it.

___ Whether I study or not has very little effect on the grades I get.

8. ___ People like me can change the course of world events by making ourselves heard.

___ It is wishful thinking to believe that anyone can influence what happens in society.

9. ___ I am the master of my fate.

___ When I see an unfortunate person, I sometimes think, "There, but for the grace of God go I."

10. ___ Getting along with people is a skill that can be learned.

___ Most people are difficult to get along with; there is no use trying to be friendly.

11. ___ I am usually a good influence on others.

___ Running around with bad company leads a person into bad ways.

12. ___ Peace of mind comes from learning how to adapt to life's stresses.

___ I would be much happier if people weren't so irritating.

SCORING YOUR SURVEY: HOW "INTERNAL" ARE YOU?

To score yourself, add up the number of choices you selected on the left-hand side. Count the number of checkmarks on the items on the left side of each pair. This total is your "internal" score. Students who took this test during the pretesting of this book received scores ranging from 6 to 12. The higher your "internal" score, the greater the control you see yourself as having over your life.

As described on page 82, students who know that they are personally responsible for many things that happen in their lives are called "high internals." They believe that the main location of what controls important forces in their lives is inside themselves.

Many other students believe that they are the helpless pawns of fate. They believe that forces influencing their lives are external to themselves. These students are called "high externals."

The point we want to make here is that both sets of attitudes are correct. Each of these attitudes is self-maintaining. The students who are high internals believe they can influence much of what happens to them. They take actions to make things happen. The results of their efforts confirm their beliefs. Students who are high externals seldom take action. They believe it won't do any good. Sure enough, most of what happens to them is determined by outside forces and other people.

The fact that you are reading this book is an indication that you are probably a person who is "internal." You know that a book such as this can provide some practical tips on how to be more effective. People who are high "externals" respond to a book like this by saying, "It won't do me any good." They are right. Their habitual way of responding to learning opportunities and chances for personal growth maintain their attitude that it doesn't do any good to try.

DEVELOPING BETTER MIND HABITS

Can a person change? Can a person develop attitudes and mind habits that lead to better results?
Yes. Practice doing what successful students do.

As we have emphasized throughout the book, there are two essential elements to success. The first is having a goal. The second is taking steps to reach the goal. Psychologist David McClelland spent many years studying those individuals who are good at setting and achieving goals. He developed a way of testing college students that accurately predicts which ones will achieve the most career success. McClelland finds that the best predictor of your future is the structure of your fantasy life. *Whatever you dwell on in your mind in a relaxed state tends to be a blueprint for your future!*

FOUR FANTASY COMPONENTS RELATED
TO GOAL ACHIEVEMENT

McClelland measures achievement motivation by asking people to tell imaginative stories to pictures that they are shown. Then the stories are examined for these four features:

1. The fictional person is working to achieve a goal, to do something better or to accomplish something that others have not.
2. The person in the story has a strong need and an emotional desire to reach the goal.
3. Reaching the goal will not be easy because of certain blocks, handicaps, or barriers which are carefully considered and examined.

105

4. The person in the story keeps searching for ways to reach the goal, may get help from others, but the main reason the goal is reached is through personal effort.

Two Examples of Achievement Thinking

The fact that you are reading this book indicates that you already have a good level of achievement motivation. To be reading this book means

1. You want to be more successful in school than you are now, or just as successful but you want to succeed more easily and efficiently.
2. You are examining various blocks, attitudes, study habits, and student behaviors that may be limiting your efforts to do better.
3. You are curious about what the field fo psychology has to offer in the way of practical information.
4. You are developing your own plans on how to be more successful in those areas where you want to do better.

At a more specific level, here's how achievement motivation thinking can be used to improve scores on essay examinations. Let's say that on your last essay examination you got 71 percent correct.

Step One is to want to do better, sincerely expect that it is possible to do better, and be willing to learn how to do better.

Step Two is to evaluate the difficulties you must cope with in order to do well on an essay test.

Step Three is to ask students who do well on essays how they prepare for such examinations. Talk to the instructor to ask for comments on where you seem to be weak and how to improve. Read this and other books on how to pass essay examinations. You will learn, for example, that recall tests (essay and fill-in) are more difficult tests of learning than recognition tests (multiple choice and true-false).

You will learn that to do well on essay tests requires you first to understand the textbook and lecture material and then to study by writing out answers to questions that are most likely to be on the test.

Step Four is to develop a study plan that gives you time to prepare for the test by writing out your answers to the questions you have listed. Then, after becoming proficient with your list, trade lists with classmates and try to write out the answers to their questions.

When taking the actual test, aim to do somewhat better than before and be *curious* about how much improvement you will show. A moderately challenging improvement from 71 percent would be about 85 percent. (High achievers are moderate risk takers. People who are trying to avoid failure would tend to set improvement goals of perhaps 75 percent of 100 percent. A goal of 75 percent might be obtained by doing no more studying than before so no risk is involved that the studying won't pay off. A goal of 100 percent is so improbable that when a low score is received there is no sense of loss—the goal was impossible anyway.)

It is important to postpone thoughts about how well you will do or not do after the test is over. Richard N. Roberts, having observed hundreds of children doing problem-solving tasks, finds that "the more competent problem solver evaluates after the task is completed, whereas the less competent child evaluates prior to task completion."[*]

The same principle holds true at the college level. Negative anticipation is related to a poor outcome. In a psychology class taught by one of the authors, for example, a student who wasn't doing well in the course wrote at the top of an essay examination "I don't do well on essay tests." Sure enough, he was successful in not doing well on the test.

If you expect not to do well on a test you will probably achieve that goal. If you expect that you can develop study habits that will improve your test scores, then you will achieve that goal.

Achieving a goal requires more than wishes or desire. Goal achievement includes desire plus a willingness to do those things that will lead to better result.

Step Five is to take time afterwards to see the relationship between what you did beforehand and the results you obtained. The checklists provided in this book are designed to help students see such relationships.

For every important area—doing well on tests and papers, taking notes, developing friendships, working better with instructors, and developing useful study habits—we've followed all the basic steps for self-motivated achievement. With gradual practice you will begin to see more clearly the relationship between improved study habits and better success in school.

Applied Imagination

One way to increase your achievement motivation is to spend time visualizing an improved situation for yourself. See places and scenes. Picture yourself there as though watching a television program. Use your imagination to carry on possible conversations. Anticipate possible difficulties and see yourself successfully coping with the difficulties. Mentally rehearse good outcomes again and again. According to Dr. Norman Vincent Peale, the way to improve your life is to "replace a negative thought with a positive thought."

"Doesn't attention to the possible blocks and barriers mean that if you have achievement motivation, you have a negative thought?"

Not at all. The person with achievement motivation is so determined to have things work out well, he or she tries to anticipate all possible difficulties and find ways to work around them.

A person with achievement motivation does not have a negative attitude, he or

[*]Richard N. Roberts, "Private Speech in Academic Problem Solving" in *The Development of Self-Regulation Through Speech*, Gail Zivin, Ed. (New York: Wiley, 1979), p. 308.

she is being practical and realistic. On the other hand, a person is not an optimist who says, "There won't be any problems, I don't want to talk about them." A naive optimist will undertake projects without pausing to think about the possibility of difficulties arising. A person with achievement motivation is both optimistic about the outcome and realistic about the negative factors involved in achieving goals.

Build Self-Esteem Gradually

"How can I be sure that I will achieve my goals?"
Here we get back to the issue of self-esteem. Self-esteem is a feeling that you have about yourself. A feeling of confidence in yourself which gradually builds up over a period of time. Nathaniel Brandon has a definition of self-esteem that helps explain this. He says, "Self-esteem is your reputation with yourself." It takes a while to build up. You have to do things that you will like yourself for and avoid doing things that you will dislike yourself for. *The way to build up confidence in yourself is to set moderately challenging goals.* As we have emphasized throughout the book, only set goals that you truly believe you can reach, using reasonable effort. Then when you reach the goal, this gives you a good experience of yourself. Your self-confidence increases, and the next time you set a slightly more challenging goal. *There is a two-way interaction between self-esteem and achieving your goals.*

Make Daydreaming Pay Off

Once you've chosen a goal for yourself, spend time visualizing yourself as having achieved it. Daydream about how people would talk to you. Imagine what positive things people will say. Visualize the pleasant reactions of instructors and employers and others who may have contact with you. See yourself walking, speaking, feeling, and talking after achieving success. Involve all the senses you can. Imagine yourself being treated to a movie or concert by someone who is impressed with your accomplishments.

Learn to Accept Praise for Accomplishments

Many school counselors see students with poor expectations who find it hard to accomplish much. Such students often feel lonely and unloved. Not because they don't have love given to them, but because people can experience only about as much love and freindship as they believe they are worth. They can only accept about as much credit as they believe they deserve.

Perhaps you have seen someone, after being complimented for doing something well, blush and argue, "It wasn't anything" or "I didn't do much," "It was nothing," or "Don't thank me, anyone could have done that." This is the same person, amazingly, who may say later, "I wish people appreciated me more."

If you want to feel appreciated, make certain you accept compliments well.

AVOID GAMES LOSERS PLAY

It is all right to feel sorry for yourself once in awhile, but if you do it frequently, you may be playing a game. A game, as explained by Eric Berne, occurs when a person follows a sequence of actions or words that manipulates others into responses that provide a hidden psychological payoff. The game is not usually fun or pleasant. The moves are superficially plausible, but the real motive is hidden. Game playing is like "conning" someone but differs in that a "con" is conscious whereas game playing usually goes on without conscious awareness.

Keep in mind that playing games is not a sign that someone is "sick," we just want to show that the games students play often have payoffs that prevent them from being successful in school. It may be that you play some games that hinder your ability to do well in school.

YES, BUT . . . .

A good example to start with is the game "Yes, but . . . ." It was the first game that Eric Berne analyzed and it lead to his development of transactional analysis.

Student: "I can't seem to concentrate."

"You could study in your room, instead of in the cafeteria."

"Yes, but it's too noisy there."

"Why don't you shut your door and play your radio?"

"Yes, but my roommate always talks to me."

"Why don't you . . . ."

"Yes, but . . . ."

On the surface, the student seems to be asking for suggestions about how to keep from being distracted. The real purpose of the interaction, however, is to prove to others that nothing they suggest is going to work.

AIN'T IT AWFUL . . . . ?

Minimartyr is walking down the hall after class and, as usual, starts a conversation by saying,

"Ain't it awful the way she loads work on us."

". . . the way she grades."

". . . how the tests are written."

". . . how the lectures are so boring."

". . . the way we have to sit on those hard seats."

WOODEN LEG

"How can anyone expect me to do well with the troubles I have. If you had the problems I have—my family and I get into these big arguments each week and I have these headaches; I lost all my notes; I can't sleep at night; I'm broke . . . ."

"I know someone who has lots of the same problems."

"My problems are worse! No one has problems as bad as mine."

HARRIED

Whirlwind takes on everything and volunteers for more. A moving dynamo of activity, Whirlwind works frantically on dozens of projects. On the verge of exhaustion, he or she charges ahead. There are meetings to attend, phone calls to make, people to see, details to arrange.

"Studying? Have to put that off until later."

Whirlwind is busy but doesn't get much accomplished.

Remember: The more goals you have the less likely you are to reach any of them.

STUPID

"Oh no! There I go again. Look how dumb I am! I always do these *stupid* things. I always find some way to foul things up! I always make some dumb mistake."

"True."

IF IT WEREN'T FOR HIM . . . .

"I could get good grades in math if it weren't for the instructor."

"I would have a good grade average if it weren't for my counselor making me take those tough courses."

"I would go to class if the instructor weren't so boring."

"I could have qualified for a scholarship if the instructor hadn't given me a C in biology."

"I could study better if it weren't for the noise at home."

Pay Attention to Repeating Problems

These games all have predictable patterns and they are repeated. The same thing happens again and again and again. The person doesn't change or find a way to deal with what happens. The gains from game playing seem to be worth more than whatever cost there may be, including being not successful as a student.

There are more games that people play. There are even games played by students who get top grades. By mentioning a few games that scholastic losers play, we have tried to show that students who would like to be more successful may unknowingly act in ways that work contrary to their chances of being successful. Blaming others for your failures is a surefire way to avoid knowing yourself and avoid learning useful lessons about life. You needn't fall into these traps. By following the suggestions outlined in *Student Success* you can have more success if you really want it.

People who blame others for their difficulties are usually described as having negative attitudes. Their theme song is "If only other people would change, my world would be a better place for me."

HOW TO REPLACE NEGATIVE ATTITUDES
WITH POSITIVE ATTITUDES

The first step toward developing more positive attitudes is to recognize the difference between positive and negative.
People with positive attitudes tend to

look for the good in a situation.
be optimistic about outcomes.
be happy about whatever good things are happening.
be pleasant people to be around.
be rarely side-tracked by irritations.
focus on getting good results.
believe that a positive expectation can improve a negative situation.

People with negative attitudes tend to

find something wrong in any situation.
be pessimistic about outcomes.
be unhappy because some good things have not happened.
believe things will eventually get worse.
be easily distracted by irritations.
be unpleasant to be around.
believe that their negative attitude is a legitimate consequence of a negative
   situation.
focus on having good intentions.

Advantages To Being Negative

We want to caution you, however, about having a negative attitude toward people with negative attitudes. For one thing, people with negative attitudes make people with positive attitudes look good. They are useful to have around. And there are many advantages to having a negative attitude. If there weren't any advantages, no one would stay negative very long!
Some advantages of a negative attitude are

you can frustrate people who would like to influence you.
people don't expect as much of you.
you get more attention.
the world is more predictable.
it's easier than being positive.
you avoid disappointment.
you avoid responsibility for things that go wrong.
you have fun playing games with people.

111

How can you tell if you have a positive or a negative attitude? If you don't know, then you probably tend to be negative. People with positive attitudes usually know that they have them. A person maintains a positive attitude pretty much out of choice. He or she is consciously aware of the existence of the attitude and how useful it is to maintain it. People who are in the middle (neither strongly positive nor strongly negative) or who tend to be negative usually have not thought much about their attitudes, and certainly they haven't considered that they have a choice about the attitudes that they hold.

Consistent with what we've said about "high externals," people with negative attitudes rarely entertain the idea that they can to anything about the attitudes that they have. As one rather negative student said, "An attitude is an attitude and you're stuck with what you've got."

Attitude Differences

We ran across several examples of attitudes when we passed our earlier drafts of this book out for review. A student with a positive attitude said, "Hey! Good! Maybe I can get more tips on how to do better in chemistry." A student with a negative attitude said, "Well, I can try some of these things, but they probably won't work for me."

Positive people tend to look for ways to improve. There is the desire to be better and an awareness that people can learn how to be better. Negative people aren't oriented toward learning and improvement. If urged to do something by external forces (other people pressuring them), they may promise to "try." But the promise "I'll try" usually signifies that they will only go through the motions for awhile. They expect to eventually drift back into acting as they always have.

Another key difference in attitude is whether or not you learn from experience. A person with a positive attitude has a positive attitude toward mistakes. As one scientist wrote, "If your experiment goes exactly as predicted, you don't learn anything. The times when you learn something are those times when your experiment does not go as predicted."

A person with a positive attitude is unhappy about making a mistake or not reaching a goal, but this person starts thinking, "What will I do the next time this happens?" Examples of positive thinking are

"The next time I'm asked a question like that . . . ."
"The next time she says that to me, I'm going to say . . . ."
"The next time I'm in a situation like this, here's what I'm going to do . . . ."

The positive person tends to focus on the future; the negative person tends to dwell on the past. This person spends a lot of time feeling sorry for what has happened.

"I would be able to study if I didn't have such a gabby roommate."

"I probably could do better in English if my high school teacher had taught me something.

"I thought I would like psychology, but the instructor bores me to death."

Do you recognize any of these mental habits in yourself? If you recognize some of the negative statements as similar to ones you make, we hope you've also recognized by now that you have a choice about how you allow your mind to react. All these reactions are *learned.* Successful people work at acquiring positive mental habits.

Let's take the example of the boring instructor. If you were turned off by a course because you didn't like the instructor, you are allowing your mind to ask the wrong question. You're letting your mind ask, "Do I like him?" The right question is, "Does he know his subject?" Whether or not he happens to have good speaking skills is irrelevant to your obtaining useful information about the subject.

For the student with a positive attitude, a boring instructor may offer a good opportunity to practice techniques on how to influence instructors to be better. (See Chapter 9.)

We don't want to mislead you into thinking that a person has to change his attitudes before his performance will improve. There is ample evidence to show that the opposite is often true. After first changing performance, a person can find that the attitude has changed. William James was one of the first to discover that changing attitudes can change behavior and that changing behavior can change attitudes. This is partly why in our book we often recommend that even though you're not quite sure that something will work, you go ahead and act as though it will work. In many instances, we will encourage you to act as successful students do. Frequently, you will find that when you begin acting as an effective and skillful person does, soon your attitudes and expectations will fall into line with your behavior.

SELF-DEVELOPMENT PROJECT: GAINING A MORE POSITIVE ATTITUDE ABOUT SCHOOL

Many of the students who show up at the centers for improving study skills have negative attitudes. They are negative about going to school, about attending classes, about teachers, and about studying. Being a person who sincerely wants to get a better education, who works at improving attitudes about school, classes, and study, is as important as learning effective studying techniques. Here is a four-week plan for gaining a more positive attitude, which has been used successfully with many hundreds of students.

STEP 1   Take several days to make up a list of the negative thoughts, feelings, and statements which occur from the time you wake up in the morning until the time you go to sleep at night. To develop a complete list, it is useful to carry a small notebook or some blank 3 X 5 cards to write down thoughts, statements, or feelings immediately after they occur. NOTE: It is important that you do not criticize yourself for having negative thoughts or statements. First we want to get an accurate picture of what exists.

STEP 2   Using the same method, write down the thoughts, feelings, and statements of a positive nature which occur for several days. This step is at the information-gathering stage, so do not yet try to emphasize or increase the number of positive thoughts or statements. Our objective here is to gain information about how frequently they occur at the present time.

STEP 3   Each day for the next 28 days, have your cards or notebook with you. As you go through the day, record each time that you say or think something which is a sign of having a positive attitude. Record this as it occurs. At the same time, keep a record of any negative thoughts, feelings, or statements that you make. During this four-week period, if you find that a negative thought or statement has occurred, then try to follow it or replace it with a more positive statement.

STEP 4   Each night, record on a chart the number of positive feelings and statements which occurred during the day and the number of negative feelings or statements which occurred. This program will help you become more aware (a) of your own thoughts, feelings, and statements and (b) of the fact that you can choose to increase or decrease thoughts, feelings, and statements which you make. Students using this program have been able to significantly increase their positive attitudes toward school, classes, and studying and have been able to decrease their negative reactions. NOTE: As you go through the program, you will find more statements and thoughts occurring to add to your original list, so feel free to revise them as you go along.

MAINTAINING A POSITIVE ATTITUDE IN NEGATIVE SITUATIONS

Maintaining a positive attitude can be difficult if one is in a negative environment. As strongly as you may be motivated to be successful, there are always a number of unmotivators working on you. Sometimes the most practical way to maintain a positive attitude is to allow yourself to fully experience all of your negative feelings for a short period of time. You can more accurately assess and cope with the factors working against you after venting your feelings. Freud saw emotional "catharsis" as a valuable step to better thinking. If you try to ignore the negative effects of various stresses, they build up and begin to burden you. To handle negative situations effectively requires that you be honest about your feelings and very clear about what it is that you are trying to handle. This means that you sometimes sit

114

you a much better chance of changing things if you don't like them the way they are. Many people spend so much time fussing about where they are that they don't see what they could do to change things. Instead of being angry, ask yourself, "Why is it good for me that this has happened?"

Create a Better Future

Pick something that you can influence and concentrate your efforts on improving it. Make your effort realistic and possible. Make it something you expect that with good effort you will be able to improve. Wishes don't count here. In the long run, it's people's expectations that are the best predictor of how well their futures will go. By accepting responsibility for yourself, choosing to work toward improving something in your life, developing a plan in which you expect to succeed, you probably can maintain a positive attitude in even the most negative of situations.

In the next chapter we'll look at a specific area for improvement: how to have more friends and get support from loved ones.

down with a pad of paper and start writing out all of the things that you have to cope with that are difficult.

A realistic positive attitude includes being able to look at the problems, the difficulties, the negative factors which have to be coped with. Take a moment now to answer this question: "By choosing to do well in school, what are some of the problems and difficulties that I have to cope with?"

Here are some of the negative factors reported to us by good students:

It takes more energy.
You work harder than poor students.
Risk of failure.
You have less time for friends than poor students.
Less chance to loaf around.
Missing some fun things because of studying for assignments or tests.
People expect more ("you get a B and they have a heart attack!").
Inability to go out for sports as often because practice interferes with studying.
Greater likelihood of being "razzed" and called "bookworm" or "egghead."
Family being upset because you don't have as much time for them.
People give you a bad time if your grades drop a little.
Some people think you're weird if you get top grades.

To this list of negative factors we would add

Being exposed to too much information too fast.
Delayed payoff for learning. The real benefits are far away and not definite. Grades are temporary motivators and are not the end goal.
Required courses of uncertain value.
Not getting enough sleep because of having to study late at night.

Perhaps as you've read these various sources of negative stress you've come up with several more of your own. There are many forces working against you, and that's exactly why we included these lists. If it were easy to be successful, more students would be.

So, what can be done?

If you make yourself aware of all the forces working against you, you will be better prepared to hold up against them. You will avoid "burnout."

Here are some suggestions about what to do to maintain a more positive attitude.

Create Your Own Support Group

Successful students associate with other successful students. If the people you associate with now do not support your efforts to be more successful, consider the advantages of finding people who will support you. You may find that it is easier to develop new friends who have the qualities you want to associate with than it is to change your old friends into being the way you would like them to be. Benjamin Franklin did this. He created a self-improvement group which met regularly for the purposes of self-development. In his autobiography, he described his "Junta" as very successful.

One way to start a self-improvement group or a support group is to organize a discussion around the use of this book. Get together with four or five other students who are reading and using it. What projects have they carried out? What results have they achieved? What have they found to be of most value?

Avoid Negative People

Successful students avoid negative students. People who are complaining, who are having problems, who are constantly being upset can drain much of your valuable energy. Avoid such people as much as you possibly can. Give minimum time and energy to their habit of experiencing pain and having problems.

Find Friends to Laugh and Play With

Successful people do not study all the time. Do anything you can to prevent your college life from getting too serious, too burdensome, and too heavy. Laughing and playing has many beneficial effects on your mental and physical health. Make a conscious effort to get into activities where you can yell or laugh or play hard and completely forget your responsibilities at school and home. If you are not doing much of this now, take another look at the recreation facilities on campus. Look for opportunities to do something just for yourself, particularly if it gives you great enjoyment.

Get Physical Workouts

Do something several times a week in which you work up a sweat. This might be bike riding, jogging, playing raquetball or tennis, swimming, or perhaps just calisthenics or stretching in your room. In any case, doing something which increases your physical tiredness helps you sleep better and rest better, which in turn helps you to study better. Physician William Glasser reports in his book *Positive Addiction* that in every instance where he finds a person who has an addiction to physical exercise, this is an individual who has more strength and energy for coping with life's stresses. Many people who handle life well do not have positive addictions. What he suggests for people who are looking for a way to handle life better, is to develop a positive addiction.

Listen to Good Music

Play some classical music and do nothing else but listen to it. Don't try to exercise good time management by also shining your shoes, writing letters, or cleaning out your desk. Sit back and totally lose yourself in the music. The word "music" stems from the activity of musing. So do it. Muse.

Try Nap Therapy

Taking naps is a wonderful way to relax and revitalize yourself. If you drive to school, try taking a nap in your car for 30 minutes or so. Take a short nap early in the evening instead of watching television before studying. Take naps on weekends if you wish. Just because you're not longer a child doesn't mean that you can't benefit from a short nap now and then.

Ignore What You Can Do Nothing About

In going over your list of those things which can contribute to your being in a negative situation, decide to stop worrying or spending any mental and emotional energy on those things that you can do nothing about. By devoting your energy to those things that you can change, you experience a much more successful life.

Go to the Counseling Center

All college students, at one time or another, have periods of feeling lonely and depressed. When this happens to you, remember that such feelings are part of being human. Regardless of how special or unique you believe your loneliness or depression is, the school employs counselors who can probably be very helpful. They won't have a miracle pill for you to get rid of unpleasant feelings, they'll have something much better. They will show you how to get through the unpleasant period while the natural emotional processes of self-healing are operating.

Even if you are reluctant to see a counselor, telephone or drop by the counseling center anyway. You can always try other solutions if you don't like the counselor. In fact you may not want to talk with a counselor at all, preferring to use other center resources. Many counseling centers have libraries of useful books and cassette tapes on how to deal with depression, get over nervousness, be less shy, and so forth.

Emotional upsets are a normal part of college life. You don't have to try to handle them by yourself. It is not a sign of strength to mask your feelings with drugs or put on a front of happiness. Emotional strength develops from feeling whatever you feel and letting another human being be close to you when things aren't working perfectly.

Choose to Be Where You Are

Successful people find value in their present circumstances. This doesn't mean that you *adjust* to your situation, it means that you *adapt* to it. To adapt means that you stay in contact with something and work to influence it to become better. Choosing to be where you are keeps you in contact with what's happening. It gives

CHAPTER 11

How to have a few good friends and gain support from your family

© 1968 United Feature Syndicate, Inc.

"Dr. James?"

"Hello, Sid, come on in."

"Dr. James, could I ask you a question?"

"Sure Sid, what is it?"

"In psychology class you teach us a lot about how to understand human behavior. But I can't find the answer to my question any place."

"What's that?"

"How do you keep from being so lonely?"

"Well, what have you tried?"

"I used to drive people places in my car—sort of a free taxi service—but that didn't work. I was moving and hauling stuff all over the place, but still no one was friends with me."

"What else have you tried?"

"For awhile I paid for everything. Cokes, hamburgers, movie tickets, popcorn, ice cream, but that kept me broke. Then I tried telling jokes. I bought a joke book and each time I was going to be with people I would memorize four or five jokes to tell."

"How did that work?"

"People laughed sometimes, but I couldn't always tell if they were laughing at me, or the joke. It didn't make anyone more friendly. It always ends up the same: they thank me for the ride or the ice cream, or laugh at the joke, and then go out with other people. I need friends too! How can I get people to like me?"

As with success in school, you have choices about how many friends you have.* Having friends is not a matter of luck, or having money, or having a great personality. Feelings of friendship develop between people as a result of a combination of variables that you can influence.

THE PROBLEM OF LONELINESS

College counselors and advisors know that a major problem for many college students comes from having very few friends. The reason why this problem has such a negative impact on students and affects their grades can be understood more clearly by looking at the hierarchy of needs described by Abraham Maslow.

This chart (see page 121) implies that the need to feel accepted and liked by people takes priority over the need to engage in personal growth and development. This relationship helps explain why it is so hard to study when you feel that no one likes you or loves you and why it is hard to read in the library while rehearsing an imaginary conversation with someone sitting nearby.

A view which is developing about the great popularity of "cults" is that the cults take care of the need for friendship and acceptance. For a person who is lonely, the invitation to join into a group and be a warmly welcomed friend is enticing.

*Note: If you have plenty of friends, skip this chapter. Or better yet, skim through it and let us know on the feedback sheet about anything else we might include. Thanks.

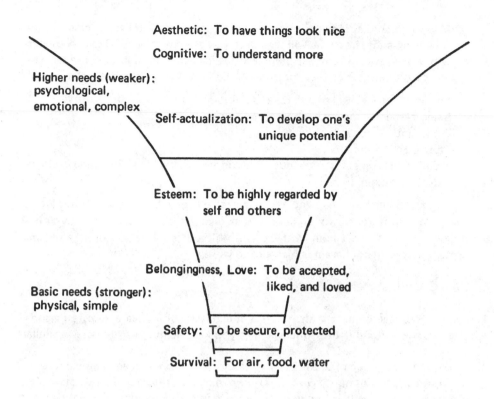

Aesthetic: To have things look nice

Cognitive: To understand more

Higher needs (weaker):
psychological,
emotional, complex

Self-actualization: To develop one's
unique potential

Esteem: To be highly regarded by
self and others

Belongingness, Love: To be accepted,
liked, and loved

Basic needs (stronger):
physical, simple

Safety: To be secure, protected

Survival: For air, food, water

Most cults involve so much of a person's total time, however, that not much is left available for pursuing a college career. There are many things you can do to increase the number of friends that you have and the amount of warm support that you have from your family. It is not necessary to struggle through school with a rather lonely existence hoping that things will get better later on.

Have Frequent Contact

Research into the sources of feelings of friendship shows that the main contributing factor is frequency of contact. That is partly why we have emphasized so often in this book that a realistic plan for being more successful in school should include frequent opportunities to spend time with friends.

Research in college dorms, in housing projects, and in neighborhoods shows a consistent relationship between feelings of friendship and how often people have contact with each other. One study, for example, of married students assigned to campus housing units found that couples living in certain apartments remained as friends more frequently than would be predicted by chance. These were people living in apartments at the foot of the stairs. Observation finally revealed that the couples were seen more frequently because the garbage cans were located near the bottom of the stairs!

Many such studies indicate that, in general, the closer you live to someone, the more likely it is that he or she will remain to you as a close friend. Once you understand how frequency of contact influences feelings of friendship, you can see why certain conditions predict that someone would have fewer close friends at school.

Living at home instead of a dorm and not joining a fraternity or sorority.

Being married to someone who is not a student.

Working full time while going to school.

Studying all of the time.

Training full time for individual athletic events, such as swimming or long-distance running.

Frequent contact is not enough to make someone feel friendly toward you. You know from your own experience that there are people with whom you had frequent contact and whom you disliked. Without contact, however, other important factors do not have much chance to work.

Be a Good Listener

People you have contact with will feel friendlier if you have a sincere personal interest in them and if they discover that you have attitudes and interests similar to theirs.

How do you accomplish this? Ask questions and listen with an open mind.

Dale Carnegie, author of *How To Win Friends and Influence People* states "You can make more friends in two months by being interested in other people than you can in two years by trying to get other people interested in you." Why should other people be interested in you if you aren't interested in them?

So, do not work at being liked. Work more at finding out what is likeable about each person that you have contact with.

Accepting versus Judging

Good listeners have a wide range of acceptance for what they learn about others. This is why so many people feel friendly toward a person who is accepting and tolerant. If we compare observing, open-minded people with those who are more judgemental in their reactions, the ranges of acceptance and rejection look like the following:

Open-minded

| accept | neutral | reject |

Judgmental

| accept | neutral | reject |

122

Notice that the open-minded person not only has a wider range of acceptance but also a wider neutral range.

This means that much of what is learned is neither accepted nor rejected. A judgmental person, even though remaining silent, eventually communicates through facial expressions, body language, and other reactions, the attitude of "no one should think that" or "that's sick."

If the person you are listening to has attitudes and opinions that you dislike, then the chances are low that you will be a good friend of that person. You can have empathy for the individual, but you probably will not have much in the way of friendship.

A quick way to become more open-minded about other people and less judgmental is to develop the habit of mentally responding "that's okay" when you learn about another person's thoughts or attitudes.

Frequency of contact with others will make very little difference and will not lead to close feelings of friendship if you constantly have a judgmental attitude about the way other people think and live their lives.

GUIDELINES FOR DEVELOPING FRIENDSHIPS

So let's say that you are more open to doing things with people, to increasing the amount of contact that you have; that you are becoming less judgmental by saying to yourself fairly frequently "that's okay." After you've done these several things, here then are some guidelines to follow that will help promote a developing friendship.

Don't start off by trying to flatter or praise the person. Too much praise has the reverse effect. People become suspicious. They are put on guard wondering if you're trying to sell something or if you might be after something.

Don't give lots of praise to everyone. Praise from a person who thinks that everyone is fantastic all the time is not valued as much as a compliment from someone who gives occasional praise when it is deserved.

Do wait until a person knows that you have seen something worthy of interest or praise before making a comment. Your praise will then be experienced as deserved, rather than as manipulated.

Do express some disagreement if you in fact disagree with another person's viewpoint. In good friendships, people can honestly and spontaneously react with a negative comment or feelings of dislike and to know that the friendship will not be lost.

Do aim at having fun with people. Don't work at being liked. Find things to laugh about, and this includes yourself. Don't take yourself too seriously. Remember, the shortest distance between two people is laughter.

GOALS IN FRIENDSHIPS

The steps and guidelines outlined above are only able to lay the groundwork for a good beginning. After you are doing the above, more subtle factors come into play. Here are some features of good friendships:

Friends feel equal to each other. Feelings of friendship cannot exist when you feel superior or inferior to someone.

Friends are comfortable being seen together, letting people know they are friends.

Friends reveal private thoughts and feelings to each other. They share personal feelings and private thoughts not usually revealed to others. Their openness with each other is natural and spontaneous. They laugh together.

Friends can be trusted with confidential information. One of the fastest ways to destroy a friendship is to tell other people about something that you've been told in confidence.

Friends accept each other as they are. If you have a close friend, you allow that person to see you as you really are. You do not contrive or attempt to manipulate the person's perceptions of you to think of you in a certain way.

Friends experience each other as unique. A friend says that no person on earth is quite like his or her close friend.

Friends have the freedom to disagree with each other. Friends can become irritated or angry if that's how they truly feel. You don't feel truly close to someone who is never angry at you. In any relationship the strong positive feelings tend to disappear if negative ones are controlled and suppressed.

Friends are not jealous of each one having other friends. A good friendship is freeing, not limiting or controlling.

FEEL WORTHY OF FRIENDSHIP

The problem of not having many friends may not be from a lack of knowledge about what to do. Neither is it usually from people not making an effort to be friendly. In some cases, the problem stems directly from the fact that an individual does not feel worthy of having friends.

Do you feel worthy of having good friends? How do you react to the person who says, "Hi! Let's go to a movie together." How do you react to the person who walks up and starts talking with you and wants to continue talking for thirty minutes or an hour? Do you get nervous and find some excuse to get away?

If so, then check back into the previous chapter and look again at those sections that had to do with improving your self image and review the steps that can be taken to expect better outcomes.

If you find yourself uncomfortable when people make efforts to be friends with you, then take a little time to sit down with a pad of paper and fill out as long a list as you can, answering this question: What are all of the good reasons why people would enjoy being friends with me? Once you can develop a more conscious understanding that it would be very nice for people to have friendships with you, you find that probably the amount of friendship you experience from people will increase.

ACTION PROJECT FOR DEVELOPING MORE FRIENDS

Select someone to test these various principles on. Choose a person that you feel equal to. Someone likely to have attitudes and interests similar to yours. To increase your chance of success, select a person who is easily available to you. Then, you'll have more opportunities to have frequent contact.

Start by having frequent, but brief, contacts with the person. Develop the habit of saying "Hi!" as you walk by. Wave to the person as you pass. Nod and smile whenever you have an opportunity. Find out the person's name and say hello, using this person's name, every time you have a chance.

As you sense feelings of friendly recognition are developing, be ready for an opportunity to ask the person one or two questions about himself or herself. Be specific. Ask, "How are your examinations going this term?" or "What do you think of the President's announcement yesterday?"

Be willing to reveal your private attitudes or feelings briefly and then quickly focus attention back onto the other person. Don't be overly quick to like a person, don't be too eager, not at first.

Be a good listener. Listen with interest and an open mind. Try to learn what it is like to be the other person. Try to discover what is unique about this individual. Then, as you find out what he or she is really like, let yourself warm up more.

Don't be overly concerned if at first you feel that you are manipulating or doing what is so obvious that the person will see through it. People will be flattered that you are making the effort. What you're doing is acting as people do who have good friends. When you conduct yourself a new way, at first you are very aware of it. But as you practice, and see that it works, then it gradually becomes a habit. You become unaware of what you're doing and it becomes more natural for you. Your goal is to concentrate less on having friends and to focus more on being a good friend to others. Remember: *The best way to have good friends is to be one!*

ACTION PROJECT FOR GAINING MORE SUPPORT
FROM OTHERS

Most students want and appreciate support from a close friend or relative. Yet students often report that they receive less praise and recognition for their academic accomplishments than they hoped for. In fact it is not uncommon for a close friend or family member to be critical or to make discouraging remarks about academic pursuits.

125

If gaining support from others is important to you, we think the following story will show how you can influence other people to change how they treat you by changing how you interact with them. As you'll see, the principles described in Chapter 8, How to Influence Your Instructors, were used by a student to gain more attention and recognition from her father.

Barbara's Story

Barbara was starting her sophomore year in nursing school when she took introductory psychology. As a course assignment she was required to do a "behavior-change project." The project involved using principles of behavioral change with a person she had frequent contact with in daily life.

Other students in the class went to work on younger sisters, neighbor children, bus drivers, talkative roommates, boyfriends who drove too fast, smokers, over-weight friends, and other available subjects. Barbara decided to use her father as the subject for her project.

Barbara's relationship with her father was very poor. She said

> We were always looking for ways to cut each other. He enjoyed saying rotten things about nurses to me. If he'd say, "good morning" to me, I'd say, "what's good about it!" If I came home from school excited about something and wanted to talk about it, he would just sit there in his chair and keep on reading. He didn't care about anything that was happening to me. Once when I was trying to talk to him about school he got up and walked out of the room. Didn't say a word. Just walked out.
>
> He is retired, so he is usually home during the day. I know he likes it, if when I'm home at lunch time, I make a bowl of soup for him. I'd go into the kitchen and make myself something. He would get his hopes up and then be disappointed when he saw I only fixed something for myself. Chocolate cake is his favorite, so when I baked something I made sure it was *not* chocolate cake.
>
> When we were assigned the project, I decided to see if I could improve my life at home. It is hard enough getting through nursing school without always having a big hassle at home. I've been dreaming about going into nursing for a long time. It's exciting! I wanted my family to care!

Barbara's Plan for Changing Her Father

Barbara decided that each time her father responded pleasantly or positively she would be pleasant to him and do something special to show her appreciation for his interest in her. The slightest positive gesture from him would be immediately attended to by her. She would try never to overlook the slightest improvement, no matter how small or weak. Her goal was to increase the number of times her father showed interest in her and the depth of his interest.

Following the procedure recommended in class, Barbara outlined these steps:

Desired project goal: Father to greet me cheerfully each morning; show interest in what is happening at school; talk with me about school.

Current level of desired behavior: Seldom looks at me or listens when I am talking about school; never asks about school.

Reinforcements to father for increase in desired behavior: Bowl of soup at lunch; bake cookies and chocolate cake; smile and say "Thanks for talking with me"; kiss on the cheek.

Three weeks later Barbara reported the results of her project to the class:

"My first chance to use a reinforcement was during a lunch time. I talked with Dad for several minutes, and he listened without looking at his magazine. I didn't try to push my luck by going on too long, so I got up and asked him if he would like for me to fix him a bowl of soup. His face brightened up. He smiled and said, 'Yes.'"

"In the morning if he said "hello" to me, I'd smile and say "hello" and kiss him on the cheek. Mornings are much more pleasant now.

"After about three times fixing him soup at lunch, he began showing more interest and would ask questions. Then one evening he asked me to tell him about a book I read, and we spent almost twenty minutes talking. I immediately got up and went out to the kitchen and baked him a batch of cookies.

"Last Friday afternoon I got home about 1:30. He got up from his chair as soon as he heard me come in and came over and said: "I've been waiting for you. I would like to know more about what you are doing in school if you have time to talk." Did I ever! We spent *two hours* talking. That is the longest my father has had a conversation with me in my whole life! It was great! He was *really* interested. When we finished I gave him a big hug, said how great it was talking with him, and went out and baked him a chocolate cake."

Barbara suddenly grew quiet. Her eyes started to water, and she struggled to hold back tears. Her voice choked up a little as she went on to say: "Something happened this morning that isn't in my written report. I was getting ready to leave for school and Dad came up and put his arms around me. He said, 'Barbara, I want to take you out to dinner next week. I want to get to know you better before it's too late.'"

Be Assertive

If you sit back and passively hope that people will go out of their way to work at being friends with you or give you praise and recognition, you are likely to be disappointed. As with other aspects of your life, once you decide to take some initiative, and to make a reasonable effort to get yourself what you would like to have, you will find that your life goes much better. One of the important lessons of life seems to be to learn how to develop friendships, how to be a good friend, and how to gain the support of other people. It could be that learning how to develop and maintain friendships and gain support will prove to be one of the most valuable abilities you learn in college.

127

SUGGESTED READINGS

Bry, Adelaide. *Friendship: How to Have a Friend and Be A Friend.* (New York: Grosset-Dunlap, 1979).

Emery, Stuart. *Actualizations: You Don't Have to Rehearse to Be Yourself.* (Garden City, N.Y.: Doubleday, Dolphin, 1978).

Hearn, Janice. *Making Friends, Keeping Friends.* (Garden City, N.Y.: Doubleday, 1979).

Charlie Shedd, ed. *You Are Somebody Special.* (New York: McGraw-Hill, 1978).

CHAPTER 12

EXPERIENCING life
AS A school

COMMENCING IN THE SCHOOL OF LIFE

Educators call graduation "commencement." Why? They want to remind graduates that the end of formal schooling is not the end of education. For the person who is a constant learner, life is a never-ending school. Everyday experiences offer many rich and valuable lessons. One of the main purposes of a good education is to teach you good learning habits.

Learning Comes from Experience

All significant learning is based on experience. You become more aware of what you've learned by asking questions and developing answers. To view life as a school means to ask questions such as:

How did they do that?
Why didn't this work?
Why did I do that?
I wonder why people do such things?
What would happen if . . . ?
How could I find out about . . . ?

To view life as a school means that you can see human faults without becoming cynical. You discover that some students cheat during tests. You discover that the instructor doesn't catch the cheating or ignores it.

Sometimes your lessons are learned by asking questions about the experience. If the experience was unpleasant, you can ask questions like "Next time, what will I do differently?" "The next time that occurs, how will I handle it?" "The next time a person does that to me, what will I say?"

Go Beyond Your Teachers

A good education will teach you how to manage your own continuing development. Good teachers will show you how to go beyond their teaching. The real excitement in learning comes when you move past the level where others can tell you what you should learn or know. Much of the excitement of being fully alive as an adult is to recapture some of the wonderful curiosity that you used to feel as a child.

You use good judgment, of course. You're not going to give your curiosity such free rein that you harm people or do things that would cause serious damage. But it's the sort of curiosity that allows you to ask a question with sincere interest, even if it might possibly embarrass you. You experiment with something and do it in a way so that if anything goes wrong, you will be the only person hurt.

People who explore, grow, and develop are people who take risks. When people try to avoid looking bad, or avoid giving a poor impression, they don't learn much.

Self-directed learning increases as you develop self-confidence and begin to sense that what is best for you is not always pleasing to others.

ARRANGING FOR SELF-ACTUALIZATION

Abraham Maslow spent many years studying people he described as "self-actualizing." As pictured on page 121, he concluded that self-actualization emerges after the more basic needs are under reasonable control. According to the hierarchy of needs, energy for learning and developing emerges automatically after you've taken care of survival, safety, friendship, and esteem needs.

How well are you doing? Are you arranging for self-actualization by taking care of other important needs?

Assessment of Needs

For each of the areas below, first rate yourself as you see things now, using this rating scale:

   (1) Very concerned about this. This is a problem area for me.
   (2) Needs improvement.
   (3) Reasonably satisfied, but could be better.
   (4) Everything is satisfactory.
   (5) In excellent shape here. Am very pleased.

Then, in the space provided, write in a statement about how you would like to have things a year from now.

Needs	At Present	Next Year
Survival: Have good physical health; good eating habits; income is enough to pay bills and rent; have time for enjoying myself.		
Safety and Security: Feel secure in job, in residence, in family and community; have some reserves and assets to fall back on in an emergency. People feel safe around me. I don't attack or threaten others.		
Acceptance and Belonging: People like me and love me; I'm close to relatives, family, and friends; get along with most neighbors; am a welcome member at church, school and in other places; I welcome others as friends.		

Needs	At Present	Next Year

Esteem: I do things that make me feel good
about myself. I like myself. Most people like
me and respect me. I learn from mistakes;
I'm open to unpleasant information and
appreciate constructive criticism. I appreciate other's accomplishments.

Self-Actualization: I ask lots of questions,
seek new experiences, and take risks. I enjoy
self-improvement. I act according to my
emotional reading of situations and by logic
and reason. Every year of my life is different
than the last. I'm very curious. I'm discovering my unique nature. I experience most
others as unique.

Self-actualizing people survive better than people whose main concerns are
safety and security. People whose fear of risk and loss prevent them from taking
new actions or having new experiences, don't survive well. They are easily threat-
ened. They are afraid they may look foolish. They clutch up when worried about
what others may think. They flounder when dealing with the unknown.

People who handle life best have a knack for turning difficulties into growth
experiences. They keep positive attitudes in negative situations. This is why viewing
life as a school is practical and useful. *When trouble develops,* it's *useful to ask questions.* Ask "What can I learn from this? Why is this good for me? What good can
come of this?"

The paradox is that by focusing in the growth direction, you survive difficulty
more capably. Perhaps you've noticed how much we've demonstrated growth reactions throughout the book. In the opening chapter we emphasized being responsible
for yourself. In the chapter on working with instructors, we suggested using difficulties with your instructor as a way to learn to handle people better. Throughout
the book, whenever any difficult situation develops, our approach has been to show
you how you can handle the difficulty in a way that makes you a stronger, more
capable person.

DEVELOPING A SURVIVOR PERSONALITY

Some people grow stronger because of difficulty. Some people emerge from hard-
ships being more capable than they ever were before. During the 1930s, for
instance, when thousands were destitute, some people found ways to be happy and
earn a living. They went against the tide and refused to be swept away by mass

despair. Using their imaginations and inner resources, they maintained a positive direction for themselves and their families during hard times.

Flexible and Adaptable

To be a survivor is to be flexible and adaptable. If you are highly flexible, you may be experienced by others as paradoxical. This means that you show what appear to be inconsistencies to an outside observer. It works like this—survivors are serious and playful; they are trusting and cautious; independent and dependent; they are selfish and unselfish.

How can a person be both? People usually are thought of as one way or another, as introverted or extroverted, for example. Yet, many people with survivor personalities show both introversion and extroversion.

People who cope well with difficulties show many such paradoxical qualities. A person most skillful at adapting and surviving has traits that work in opposition to each other. Such a person is both gentle and tough, mature and childlike, serious and humorous, friendly and distant cowardly and courageous, lazy and hard-working, quiet and talkative, impulsive and thorough. A person who can be only one way, only serious, for example, is greatly restricted in what he or she can do. This means that the more pairs of these opposing or paradoxical traits that you have, the more you tend to show qualities of having a survivor personality.

To have these paradoxical traits is to be "and" rather that "this way but not that." You are proud *and* humble, cooperative *and* rebellious.

Inner Complexity

The list given above is not intended to be complete. The more the pairs of paradoxical traits that are a natural part of you, then the more complex you are, and thus more successful at dealing with any situation that develops.

What is the relationship between being a complex person and surviving? People who deal with systems generally hold the view that when two systems interact, the more complex one remains in control. Computer programmers, top sales people, and professional football teams all use this principle.

The Curiosity Habit

Being complex is not enough, however. In any difficult situation, it is essential, first, to be very open to quickly assess and understand what is occurring. Second, it is very important that you have the attitude of acting in ways that will have things work out well. Being open to quickly read, assess, and respond to what is occuring is an ingrained habit. It develops as a result of a lifetime of playful curiosity. This sort of curiosity gives a person much experience with dealing with unexpected developments, with stumbling into unknown circumstances, with being open to deal with bewildering situations. Survivors are drawn to the unusual, the complicated, and the mysterious. Thus, when a difficulty develops which one has not caused, the habit of being open to the new and unfamiliar predisposes you to quickly find out what is happening.

Things Working Well

People with survivor personalities need to have things work well. This means that from the moment of quickly determining what a new and unexpected development is, you are looking for a solution.

In contrast, some people are oriented toward having things go wrong. They convert difficulties into the experience of being victimized. When problems develop, they respond to the circumstances in a way so that they can get people sorry for them and pity them for having such a tragedy occur.

Survivor habits and victim habits can become so deeply ingrained people don't realize how much they make choices in responding to circumstances. Needing to have things work well is a part of being constantly open to looking for new and better solutions. Having things work well can mean giving up old assumptions and beliefs. Thus, another aspect of having a survivor personality is one of constantly asking questions to confirm how accurate your knowledge is. When a better way of perceiving or doing things comes along, people with survivor personalities adopt them.

Nonjudgmental Learning and Creativity

The ability to survive situations depends upon being able to read them accurately. Reading situations accurately results from having a nonjudgmental way of viewing the world. To be nonjudgmental is to absorb information about what exists. A judgmental attitude, on the other hand, means to quickly condemn or find something wrong at the first impression. Judgmental thinking is to quickly view things as right or wrong, to quickly think of people as being good or bad.

People who demonstrate judgmental thinking exhibit what psychologists call "premature perceptual closure." When someone begins to make a statement, judgmental thinking is to quickly decide what the statement is going to be and pass judgment on the statement. People who demonstrate judgmental thinking usually are described as having closed minds. They avoid empathy. They avoid learning how others view things. They translate much of what occurs in their world into simple categories and labels. Such thinking works directly contrary to good learning.

People with survivor personalities learn about the world without judging it. They expect human beings to be human. They expect each human being to be unique and have an individual perspective. They absorb information about what exists just for the sake of knowing.

Research into creativity shows that people who score highest on creativity tests are people who are not judgmental. Individuals who score the lowest on tests of creativity are people who have strongly judgmental ways of thinking. To be creative is to come up with unusual ideas that work.

By understanding the relationship between nonjudgmental thinking and creativity, the survivor pattern becomes more clear. People with the survivor personality are very complex. You're never quite sure what they are going to do in any situation. Yet, because they read the situations quickly and accurately and have the intention of having things work out well, their solutions are often creative.

Hunches and Intuition

Associated with the quality of creativity is an awareness of subtle inner feelings. Sometimes survivors sense that something's wrong without knowing what it is. A tight stomach or an uneasy feeling can alert them. These feelings can be set off by anything, a person's tone of voice, something not said, a group's quietness, anything at all that doesn't fit.

In the classroom, someone with a survivor orientation will listen to what the instructor says, and also monitor whether or not the information being presented "feels right." If the information feels right, the survivor will abosrb and make good use of it. On the other hand, if it doesn't feel right, there may be several alternatives, such as those we have described in earlier chapters. One of the alternatives is merely to take into account those things that the instructor believes are true, even if you don't believe that they are. Or you can speak up and challenge the instructor, based upon your own experience and your own view of things.

The ability to read and respond to subtle inner feelings gives survivors an ability to follow hunches. In general, women are better at this than men. Women are known for their intuition. This is no accident, because women are usually raised with emotions as an important part of their lives.

Guided by Reason and Feeling

Survival often results from allowing one's self to be guided by feelings. A survivor's actions are not controlled by either emotions or logic. Survivors are influenced by both. There is a harmonious interaction between mind and emotions. With survivors, when emotions are likely to become disruptive, the objective mind can take over and maintain control. When more relaxed survival may result from scanning one's emotions for clues as to what is right or wrong.

As you may learn in psychology, each of us has two brains. The right brain seems to be where nonverbal, emotional, musical, visual, intuitive, irrational, metaphorical thinking takes place. The left brain seems to be where logical, rational, sequential, verbal, time oriented, objective thinking takes place. Survivors are people who use both brains.

Empathy for Others

The people who survive best in a variety of situations have good empathy for others. They can quickly "read" the emotional states, attitudes, and perceptions of others. They can step outside of their own feelings and perceptions to take into account the feelings and perceptions of others, even when disliked.

The empathy of survivors is not that of a weak, easily hurt "bleeding heart." It is more like the empathy of a defense attorney who must accurately understand the case against his or her client in order to prepare a good defense. Their empathy is not restricted to having a feeling for people who are experiencing difficulty or enjoyment. It includes having an understanding for people who live and think in disliked ways.

The attitude present in the empathy described here is "whether I enjoy you or dislike you, I am going to understand you as well as you understand yourself—and maybe even better." With this kind of empathy some survivors can be in such good control that they joke and play with their attackers.

Humor Makes the Difference

The ability to laugh and joke during a crisis is very practical. Laughing has a direct effect on one's ability to solve problems efficiently and deal with situations. Examples can be seen on television or in the movies. "Hawkeye" in the television series "M.A.S.H." is an excellent example. Writer Erma Bombeck reacts to events in her life with the humor typical of people with survivor personalities.

Why does humor help? Laughing reduces tension. Creative problem solving, accurate thinking, and good physical coordination are best in moderate emotional states. In athletics, the coach of a football team wants the linemen worked up to a high emotional state. In sports such as basketball, tennis, or baseball, a more moderate level of emotional arousal leads to better performance.

The humor used by "survivors" is directed toward the immediate situation. It is aimed at playing with the situation and poking fun at it. It is as though the person has the attitude, "I am bigger than this situation. This is my toy. I am going to play with it."

The person seems to be asking, "How does this look from a different point of view? What would happen if I turned it upside down? What if the reverse were true? What unusual things exist here?" By playing with the situation and toying with it, the person keeps from being overwhelmed and at the same time is likely to come up with a way to survive.

Sayings Are Useful

An alternative to humor is to repeat a saying. Several typical sayings are "When the going gets tough, the tough get going" or "Every cloud has a silver lining" or "In the grand scheme of things, how much does this really count?" When handling an emergency, a person with a survival personality works to survive and turns the situation around so that something good can be salvaged.

It Isn't the Event, It's Your Reaction to It

People with survivor personalities rarely remain upset about what has been lost. They do not remain distressed when things have gone bad. They focus on the future. They know that nothing can be done now about what has happened. They accept responsibility for turning things around. They accept reality as it is. They accept responsibility for their reactions to conditions.

Martha Washington once said,

"I am still determined to be cheerful and to be happy in whatever situation I may be—for I have also learned from experience that the greater part of our happiness or misery depends upon our dispositions and not upon our circumstances."

BE RESPONSIBLE FOR YOUR HABITS

As we stated at the beginning, this is a book about useful habits. Throughout the chapters we've highlighted habits to develop—being responsible for yourself, using the SQ4R study steps, taking notes, using study schedules, preparing for tests, writing papers, and doing what successful students do.

Because a lack of friends can interfere with doing well in school we included a chapter on ways to have more friends, by developing habits that lead to good friendships.

Attitudes are habits. When necessary we've shown how attitudes (mental and emotional habits) toward school, instructors, and life in general can help or hinder you. And now in this last chapter we've given attention to personality habits which can promote self-actualization and surviving on your own by making life the best school of all.

A Practical Self-Improvement Plan

Habits to take time to develop, however. And you don't acquire them by merely reading about habits and thinking that certain ones would be nice to have. To have useful habits you need to devise a plan in which you consciously work at doing those things you wish to have occurring automatically.

Benjamin Franklin discovered how difficult it can be to develop new habits when he was in his 20s. As we mentioned in Chapter 1, after Franklin was frustrated in his efforts to improve himself, he concluded that "contrary habits must be broken and good ones acquired and established." He spent some time thinking about how he could develop desired habits. After careful thought, he concluded that habits occur when a person is not paying attention and that the number of actions a person can pay attention to is limited. Keeping this in mind, Franklin contrived the following method.

First he made a long list of the virtues that various writers, speakers, preachers, and others had put forth as desirable qualities. Then he reduced the list to what seemed to be the most basic virtues:

Temperance   Sincerity
Silence   Justice

Order	Moderation
Resolution	Cleanliness
Frugality	Tranquility
Industry	Chastity
	Humility

For each virtue, he wrote out a short statement to clarify its meaning:

Temperance: Eat not to dullness, drink not to elevation.

Silence: Speak not but what may benefit others or yourself. Avoid trifling conversation.

Humility: Imitate Jesus and Socrates.

Then Franklin took a blank book and assigned one page to each of the virtues. He put seven columns on each page, one for each day of the week. Down the left-hand margin, he put the initial letters of all thirteen virtues.

TEMPERANCE

Eat not to Temptation
Drink not to Elevation

	Sunday	Monday	Tuesday	Wednesday	Thursday	Friday	Saturday
T							
S							
O							
R							
F							
I							
S							
J							
M							
Cl							
T							
Ch							
H							

His plan was to "give a week's strict attention to each of the virtues successively. Thus, in my first week, my great guard was to avoid even the least offense against temperance, leaving the other virtues to their ordinary chance, marking every evening the faults of the day."

He saw his plan as similar to that by which a gardener works. The gardener does not try to pull out all the weeds from all the flower beds at once, "but works on one of the beds at a time and, having accomplished the first, proceeds to the second."

Franklin reasoned that, if he concentrated his entire effort on only one virtue at a time and kept at it for an entire week, then some of that effort should carry over out of habit into the next week, while he was concentrating his conscious effort on such the next virtue. He checked every virtue every evening merely to observe the status of that virtue in regard to its presence or absence in his habits. He did not judge himself wrong or hold himself responsible for any of the virtues that he was not working on that week. If he slipped up, he merely observed that he did so.

He checked his book nightly and placed a mark wherever he had slipped up. His goal was to go through the list over and over until, after "a number of courses, I should be happy in viewing a clean book after 13 weeks' daily examination." Thereafter he went through the sequence four times. The next year once, and later only once every several years.

Habits Developed Early in Life Yield Many Benefits

Some 50 years later Franklin wrote about his habit plan "On the whole, tho' I never arrived at the perfection I had been so ambitious of obtaining but fell far short of it, yet I was by the endeavor a better and a happier man than I otherwise should have been if I had not attempted it . . . ." And . . . "It may be well my posterity should be informed that to this artifice, with the blessing of God, their ancestor owed the constant felicity of his life down to his seventy-ninth year, in which this is written."

The younger you are when you develop useful habits the bigger the payoff will be. As you grow older it becomes more difficult to stop bad habits and learn new ones. Here is what the great psychologist William James wrote about habits:

Could the young but realize how soon they will become mere walking bundles of habits, they would give more heed to their conduct while in the plastic state . . . . Let no youth have any anxiety about the upshot of his education . . . . If he keeps faithfully busy . . . he may safely leave the final result to itself. He can with perfect certainty count on waking up some fine morning, to find himself one of the competent ones of his generation.

Young people should know this truth in advance. The ignorance of it has probably engendered more discouragement and faint-heartedness in youths embarking on arduous careers than all other causes put together. (*Principles of Psychology* by William James. Holt, 1890.)

Being Responsible for Yourself

Are you worth a few minutes of your own time? Would you be able to develop a habit improvement plan for yourself if you really wanted to?

The next step is up to you. We, Tim and Al, could at this point present a list of useful habits from the various chapters but we won't. Such a list would be our list and not yours.

For a self-improvement plan to work you have to make it up for yourself. We recommend that you do what Franklin did. Make up a list of those behaviors and attitudes which you truly would like to acquire as habits. Write out a short behavioral description of each habit in practice. Set modest goals and expect to take years to reach them. Spend a few minutes each day recording how well you have done and reflect on your new experiences.

Remember: The best investment you will ever make is in yourself. Are you ready to commence?

SUGGESTED READING

The Farther Reaches of Human Nature by Abraham Maslow (New York: Viking, 1971). Maslow selected the articles which make up this book, his last. Although he was unable to edit the manustript before he died, it serves as an inspiring and thought-provoking description of the complex forces guiding humans to their highest potential.

Growth Psychology: Models of the Healthy Personality by Duane Schultz (New York: Van Nostrand Reinhold, 1977). Schultz compares the views of six noted experts. He summarizes and compares the views of the healthy adult personality as described by Allport, Rogers, Fromm, Maslow, Jung, Frankl, and Perls. The book is well written and stimulating in its questions and issues. This book would be an excellent choice for a self-development group.

YOUR COLLEGE ORIENTATION

BE ASSERTIVE ABOUT ORIENTATION

Your college tries to inform you of every facility and service available to you. Regardless of how hard the orientation leaders try, they are bound to overlook something. This appendix describes the college support services and facilities you should know about. You can use this appendix as your checklist. As you go through whatever form of orientation your college offers, become familiar with all the services and facilities we list that are offered by your college.

If you have completed an orientation program, use this appendix to review your knowledge of campus services. Orientation is a continuous process throughout your matriculation in college. You will need the use of various resources. Make sure you know what they offer and where they are located.

If during your orientation it appears to you that a service or facility isn't going to be mentioned, ask about it. If you still don't find out all you want to know, make sure you search out more information on your own.

Be assertive. Don't stay away from a support service because of rumors or negative advice.

If possible, pay a visit to every service or facility to check it out. For example, most colleges have Learning Skills Centers and Writing Improvement Centers. Often, to find out about what these support services can offer you, you'll need to stop in and have a chat with a staff member. DON'T HESITATE. You'll usually find that staff members of college support services are trying to think up ways to insure that students make use of their services.

Take a stroll over to the Intramural Sports Center, the Office of Financial Aid, or to any one of the libraries on campus. You may pick up a few ideas about ways in which you want to spend your time on campus. You may learn about financial help you didn't know was available to students such as yourself.

TAKE THE TOUR

Most colleges provide guided tours during your orientation program. By all means, take advantage of your orientation tour wherever and whenever it occurs.

During your orientation program, you'll probably be provided with loads of information about the programs, facilities, and opportunities available at your college. Amongst the information, you'll often find a "survival kit," which is usually provided by the college admissions office. Your packet should explain procedures for registration and describe various services and facilities available to you.

If you look around campus, you will probably find free copies of the college newspaper. College newspapers often put out a special "orientation edition" to acquaint new students with the various activities and goings on on campus.

The checklist of college services and activities we've provided is typical of what you'd often find at a larger school. Whether your college has more or fewer of the places we've listed, use our list as a starting point as you acquaint yourself with your campus. The more quickly you become familiar with your campus, the more you will feel at home. Learn why certain offices and facilities exist, even if you don't use them now. At some point it may be to your advangage to know where and why most offices and services exist.

College Orientation Checklist

DEAN OF STUDENTS
This is the office to contact if you have any questions or difficulties that are not immediately handled some place else. The Dean of Students is responsible for seeing that you are well taken care of in school and that any problems you have can be solved. It is likely that if you go to the Dean of Students' office you will be referred to another office some place else. That's okay. Their job is to know where to send you and how to find the answers that you want to find.

REGISTRAR
The Registrar's office is responsible for keeping all academic records. This is the office where you go if you are confused about a grade that you have received or which may have recorded incorrectly. If you have taken classes elsewhere, at any time in the past, the Registrar's office can give you information on how to claim credit and obtain documentation so that it will apply to your program. After you graduate, the Registrar's office provides transcripts which may be requested at future times.

ACTIVITY CENTER OR STUDENT UNION

Here is where the students hang out. You will find cafeterias, art displays, television rooms, reading rooms, possibly a bowling alley, a barber shop, ping pong tables, and pool tables. The Student Union on every campus is unique, so take time to walk around and familiarize yourself with this building. On the bulletin boards you will find announcements for theater offerings and for the college film offerings. Student groups frequently organize film festivals which show films not available in the regular theaters in your community.

TRANSPORTATION OFFICE

If you have to commute to school you may need a permit to park in the campus parking lots. Be sure to find out about carpools and university busses as an alternative to driving your own car each day.

FINANCIAL AID OFFICE

Scholarships are only one form of aid or financial support offered to students. There are organizations which provide grants to needy students. A grant is an outright gift, which does not have to be repaid. In some instances, for a person who is without funds, the college may have a way to reduce tuition fees. Most students qualify for loans at very low interest rates. These funds are provided by the Federal Government, and by other sources. If you are a veteran, you probably know about your GI benefits, provided by the Federal Government, but do you also know that schooling benefits may be provided by your state? The Office of Financial Aid can tell you if you qualify. Another source of funds is through student employment, or "work-study programs." There are many jobs available on campus for students who need income. These jobs don't pay a great deal, but they are on campus and are usually flexible to fit with the student's class schedule.

CASHIER'S OFFICE

All monetary matters involving tuition are handled here. *Note:* The cashier's office may cash checks for any person with a valid student body I.D. card.

EMPLOYMENT OFFICE

A separate office usually exists to coordinate job offers from local employers with students who are looking for off-campus work. There are many jobs in every community which fit perfectly with being a student. These range from part-time sales work, where you work at hours of your own choosing, to some sort of night work, where you mainly have to sit and watch equipment running.

STUDENT ADVISORS

Your school will have people available to provide academic counseling. This would be to provide information on class schedules, on different courses required for certain majors, your eligibility for certain programs, and such. This activity might be included within the Dean of Students' office but not necessarily.

COUNSELING CENTER/CAREER COUNSELING

These services may be separate or combined. Each has professional counselors available. These counselors are prepared to have private sessions with students who need to talk about more personal matters, when certain stresses and problems become more difficult than a person can cope with. The psychologists and/or counselors who work in these centers are especially trained to deal with student problems.

HEALTH SERVICE

Every campus has a medical unit of some kind available for emergency medical care and treatment. It is useful to know where this center is and what services are provided before you need any help from them.

The health service on your campus is probably a resource for information, programs, and services on human sexuality, birth control, prevention of venereal disease, and so on. The health service may also have people trained to deal with alcohol and drug abuse problems.

CAMPUS SECURITY

Find out how to get help from campus security in case of an emergency. They are the people to call first when any sort of help from police is needed. TIP: Make friends with the security officers. They appreciate it.

STUDENT HOUSING

Your school may provide student housing in its own dormitories. It will also coordinate placement of students into private homes and facilities that exist in the nearby area. Many landlords will register the availability of housing with this office.

STUDY SKILLS CENTER

This center is staffed with specialists on teaching people how to read faster, remember better, pass tests more easily, and, in general, to succeed in the academic aspects of school. Improving study skills often is the solution to dealing with "emotional problems."

LIBRARY

Visit the library and take some time to walk through it. You will find that all the stacks are open. You can go almost any place in the library and see what is available. You will notice that in the library there are many, many desks and study areas available. You might consider picking a spot in the library for your regular place to study.

Librarians usually enjoy telling people about all the library services. Take advantage of this good will.

Plan to learn, as soon as possible, about how to use the microfilm equipment. It is not as complicated as it may look to you. Many library materials are stored on microfilm, so it is important to learn what to do if you need to use the equipment.

MUSEUMS AND ARCHIVES

Many colleges and universities have received museums and archives from private donors. These collections may be housed in their own buildings somewhere near campus. Find out about these unusual opportunities. The staff will appreciate your interest and you may get much more of an education by exploring these places than you expect.

LEARNING CENTER

Many schools have established special centers where you go in order to learn a specific subject. You check in and tell the person in charge what you want. You will then likely be assigned to a booth with a set of earphones, a television monitor, or a computer terminal. You work at your own speed at the lesson you are there to learn or complete and can stay with it as long as you wish. The person in charge will be glad to explain to you how everything works.

WOMEN'S CENTER

Women returning to school, particularly those with families, often have more difficulties to cope with than most men do. To assist women with the unique problems that they must cope with, most schools have established a women's center. This is staffed by very capable and experienced women who are particularly skilled at helping other women cope with the problems they face in being students.

ADULT CENTER

This may be called the Seniors' Center or Gray Panthers' Office. Most schools now have at least a room where the older student can go to get information about any problems or concerns or questions that may come up.

SPORTS CENTER

Be sure to check the sports facility. As a student, you have access at certain times to the gymnasium, to the swimming pool, to the racquet ball courts, and tennis courts. Take your time to inquire, because having a nice swim between classes some day might be exactly the right thing for you. There will be an exercise room which you can use when available and there may be a track for jogging, basketball courts, and other possibilities for exercise.

DAY CARE CENTER

If you have preschool children, the college may be providing day care so that you can bring the child to school with you and for a low fee have the child cared for and fed by professionals while you are in school. This may be for all day or only for several hours.

BOOKSTORE

Take some time to go through the bookstore. Browse around to see where different books are located. Usually the front part of the store contains what is called "trade" books. These are books available to the general public and available in almost all bookstores. At the back of the store you probably will find the textbook section. The books will be arranged on shelves listed by course numbers within the different departments of the college. The bookstore will probably have ordered and stocked for courses that you will be taking. Instructors must place their orders several months before classes start so textbooks are available when you arrive.

Note: After registering for your courses, it is wise to purchase your textbooks right away. The bookstores have the texts arranged by course number and the instructor's name. If you wait until the first class meeting to hear the instructor tell you what to buy, the bookstore might be sold out. Also, if the instructor is using the same textbook again this year, you may find used copies of the book available. Be careful to purchase only the most recent edition of a textbook, however. Using the third edition of a textbook when the instructor has now switched to the fourth edition, will not be acceptable.

AROUND CAMPUS

As you travel around campus, you will encounter small groups of students encouraging you to join in their activities. You will find activity groups that are interested in having you become a jogger, hiker, bike rider, chess player, and perhaps a player of "new age" games. You may be invited to join the school choir or band. There are many action groups on campus which will seek your support. Be prepared to have students ask you to sign petitions, to support the development of solar energy, to save whales, to mobilize efforts to fight world hunger, to stop the development of nuclear power plants, to fight the dumping of poisonous waste materials into the earth and water, to free people who are being jailed or are being held hostage, to control the world's population explosion, to control animal population through neuter and spay programs. Whether you support any of these activities or not, the fact is, they are a part of campus life today.

During your tour, find out how to qualify for the Dean's honors list and what it would take to qualify for Phi Beta Kappa. Consider setting your goals high. You may be more capable than you realize! Be active in finding out every thing you can about your school.

Remember: *The entire school exists to assist you in succeeding in getting the education you want!* Take time now, before you get into your academic program, to get acquainted with your school. You will feel more comfortable more quickly, become more fully absorbed in classes, and enjoy the excitement of learning and discovering new ideas without being confused about what's going on around you.

appendix B

A CONVERSATION WITH THE AUTHORS

Note: In 1975 the first edition of this book was written with Tim and Al mailing chapters back and forth to each other from Providence, Rhode Island, and Portland, Oregon. After the book was completed, they got together in Michigan at the home of a mutual friend, James V. McConnell, to talk about the book. Their conversation was recorded and we have reproduced it here because of the perspective it gives to the *Student Success* book.

Al: Tim, I've been waiting for months to ask you this question.

Tim: What?

Al: I've been reading all these chapters you've written about generating questions, using charts, schedules, checklists, and so forth, and I want to know, *truthfully now,* did you do all this when you were in school?

Tim: No, I didn't. I have to admit I did *not* do all this when I was in school. When I was in school, the first two years of my undergraduate existence I would read and reread and reread all the chapters . . . . I would read over my notes again and again and I would periodically try to figure out from the books what questions might be on the tests. Basically, I was a really lousy student. I probably spent roughly two or three times too much time studying.

Al: What changed all that?

Tim: When I got into my junior year, I started taking a lot of courses where we knew the instructors gave the same tests year after year. So I went about getting old tests and I found out that when I practiced answering all the questions out of them that I did very well in the courses. My grade point went up. It went up from about a C+ average when I was in the first two years. My junior year I had brought it up to close to a B average. By my senior year, it was better than a B average. In my late junior and senior year I spent probably a third of the amount of time studying that I used to spend because I finally realized most of the courses required just answering questions that I could predict from a variety of sources of information. Graduate school became even more of that because I started working at the University Reading Service and I taught a lot of courses in reading improvement there. I taught people of different age ranges, began using these techniques in my own graduate courses, and worked with a lot of students who were having problems. So, to answer your question, I didn't at first. I was a lousy student. I spent far too much time studying, was very, very unhappy, considered dropping out of school several times, hardly dated at all my first two years, and spent a lot of time going over the same information time and time again. It became a very dull and boring existence and I was very displeased with school.

Al: That was my experience very much, too. At the end of my sophomore year, I had a GPA of about 2.1. I saw the other students were getting more out of school than I was . . . .

Tim: Right.

Al: . . . so I joined the service. I went in for three years in order to try to figure out what I wanted to do with my life and what I wanted to get out of my schooling, just to grow up a little bit. So, after three years, I went back to school and gradually began to learn ways of getting better grades. It was a slow process. I've been thinking back to the things that influenced me and one of the key things came right when I was a junior and I first started back in at school. I went to talk to my psych professor about why I didn't seem to be doing well at school and why studying was hard and all that. And he said, "You ought to accept the fact that studying can be hard work. To some of us it can be just as hard as physical labor. Once you face up to that reality, then it's not so difficult to deal with. Studying isn't always fun." I approached it more like, occasionally I had to do some hard work, and it was a lot easier. In fact, I got a 4.0 the next semester.

Tim: It's very interesting how many people just sort of say, "Forget it, I'm gonna quit." They go off to do something else, like work in a garage or travel to the southwest or whatever it might be because they think, "When I come back, I'll be more mature and I'll be ready to study." I found with myself, I remember in my sophomore year I took a trip to another college down south where I thought it would be easier than the University of Michigan, which is a real break-neck sort of school. I found they required you to do the same type of work under the same types of conditions. It was just that no school was that much different from any other. Maybe different calibers of students were in different schools, but the schools were basically the same. They are all tough. The community college in my home town was probably tougher than where I was going to school.

Al: Yeah, I found that also. I taught some psych classes in nursing schools and what happens is that a number of high school graduates choose to go into nursing because they feel that they don't want to get into the academic grind of the university. And what they discover in nursing school is even a *tougher* studying situation. They have to master chemistry and physiology and neurology and anatomy and diseases and medicines . . . pharmacology. They do laboratory work and for many of them it's just so overwhelming that they actually would have had it easier, as far as studying goes, if they had gone to the university.

Tim: That's quite true. I came back after this trip and I said, "Well, what it amounts to is I've got to become a better student. I have got to quit making up excuses about how teachers don't like me, or how this school's designed to get rid of the students or hurt people and all that. All of these soft feeling philosophies about how people are out to get you. The paranoid dilemma a lot of students get into about, "Well, because they are not handing me these grades on a silver platter and making me work, there must be some Utopian academic community where we just sit around and talk and philosophize, where we are graded on our intentions rather than our product.'"

Al: There are some students who will play that game. There are some bright students. They will go around acting like they never study at all and they're always playing bridge, sitting out in the sunshine reading a paperback book or having coffee someplace, out on their bikes or backpacking perhaps. And then they come in and they get an A in the course and you wonder how in the heck did they do that. Part of it is that they are smart enough to figure out what it takes to get a good grade in the course. Like you mentioned about picking up your GPA, mine went exactly the same way. I had a 2.1 in my sophomore year and I went in the service for three years. Then I came back. By the end of my junior year I had about a 2.9, and by the time I graduated it was well over 3.0. In fact, like you said, learning to predict questions on the exam?

Tim: Yes.

Al: I had one class I took in my senior year; by that time I knew this psych prof well and how his mind worked. I was taking this required course, a two-hour required course, and I purchased the textbook for the course, glanced through it to see what it was like. I knew from past experience this professor never asked questions on the final exam that came from his lecture notes. All he asked were questions from the textbook and I knew the kind of question he asked. So I did not do any studying all year long until final exam week. I finished a final in the morning, went back and had lunch and then I had two hours from the end of lunch until my final for this particular course. And in two hours I went through the book, memorized what I knew he would ask on the test, went in, took the final, got an A on the test, got an A in the course, and to this day I have no idea what that course was or what the textbook was! But it was a challenge. I was kind of testing out my philosophy, my knowledge. But I used that time in more productive ways. I really didn't care about that course. I needed the hours for my major so I used my time to do other things I really enjoyed more.

Tim: Now and then you find that a course is not all that valuable but you have to take it. It is, in your estimation, a waste of time! This is where these techniques stand out most to me. You've really got to figure out what the instructor wants and give it to him with the least strain on your part.

Al: Did you always attend classes? I always did; I never cut classes.

Tim: No, never. I was very fearful of the consequences. I don't see that in students today like I used to see it.

Al: And when I'm teaching now, actually if a student is unhappy about being in a course . . . and let's say it's a required introductory class . . . I would just as soon have them stay away. So myself, I don't care if they cut. Although I do hold them responsible for whatever is presented in the classroom and they are going to be tested on that.

Tim: Exactly . . . . One of the things I don't want students to feel, is that we are just trying to teach them how to get good grades. To me grades mean very little. I'm really concerned about what you can do after you get out of the class. I have been convinced by seeing results of people studying this way that they have more time to do things that they want, they have a better comprehension of what they really want to know, and they have done it under a much more rewarding system because there's such great predictability that if you study in this way, you will learn the answers to questions which you think are important and somebody else thinks they are important. And you still have time to go off in other directions that your instructor doesn't think are so important, but you think are important.

Al: I think, Tim, that is why you and I have gotten along so well in writing this book. I believe very much the same thing. What we are aiming at is teaching a person how to be in better control of her own education, and we are setting it up in a way that there is also the correlated advantage of being able to get better grades in classes. But the key thing is managing your own education. I do some workshops in personal growth and self-development and things like that, and one of the central points I try to drive home is that the key to self-actualization is learning how to ask good questions.

Tim: Right.

Al: Because only you can discover your own potential. To do that takes asking questions. Questions are the path ot the unknown. That's the route. So this thing of teaching the person how to develop himself more quickly and be in charge of that by asking questions all fits.

Tim: I have another goal, too, and I guess that's the sort of thing that parents run into with their children. You know, you always have your parents telling you, "Well, do it this way, because I learned the hard way and the way you're going is not the way to go." And you seldom believe it. You say, "I'll go my way, because I think it's right" and then later on you may say, "I wish I'd done what my parents told me." Time and time again in my own experiences, I've gone through this very painful process of not sitting down and asking these questions before I take each course or each time before I study for a course. What do I want to get out of this time in my life? What will I be able to do after this period of time? What questions will I be able to answer?, etc. Many students just go to a class and say, "Well, this is going to be another hour of time that I pass towards getting my degree." If that's the case, to me, time is all you have and you're just wasting it.

Al: Yes, that fits. That's why I included that section about attitudes. That was pretty much my approach. If I was sitting in a required course, I assumed immediately that there had to be a very good reason why a lot of people running the educational system decided that this particular topic was of such importance they were going to *require* that each student go through it. They wouldn't even make it an elective opportunity. So, if it was required, I figured that that was a vote of confidence for the course rather than a hassle of some kind.

Tim: I would like to save a lot of the students who read this book, all the time that is wasted, when they go around and say, "I really hate going to school." You know there are so many good things to do in college and the fact is, that you could spend your time doing them and not going to class and possibly be better off. And I knew a lot of guys who did that, who came to school and said, "Look, there are a lot of other things at this college which are considered intramural activities or pastimes you can take part in when you are not studying. In fact, I think they are more beneficial things for me to be doing, such as belonging to organizations or clubs or activities or whatever it might be." I'm not saying they were right or wrong, but, by gosh, they did learn to get as much out of their courses as they could as quickly as possible so that they could go on to do more important things for themselves. If that is what you want to choose as your goal in college, *fine,* but don't be hollering and screaming about how you would like to be able to do those things but you can't because you have to spend all your time studying. I know how to help people study. We have told them how and if they do it, they'll be a lot better off.

Al: What about this other thing of peer group pressures? There are certain norms, and they're stronger at some schools than others and certain groups within schools, not to get good grades. For example, I was reading in *Time* magazine recently about one of these English members of Parliament who was in trouble and they gave a brief background of his career, military record, and his schooling. It said, "He got gentlemen's grades at Cambridge," which means that, at one time if you were a gentleman and you went to Cambridge, the tradition was to not try to get top grades, but to get a C average. That is what a "gentleman" got because there were other more important things than just studying to get grades. Sometimes they say at school "Get the Gentlemen's C in the course." Your peer group will put pressure on you if you get an A in the course, like you are not quite one of the group if you get that kind of grade. That can be a tough thing for some students to deal with. Sometimes it operates on a person without the person realizing it. They just figure this is the way it is.

Tim: I haven't seen a lot of that. I have seen it more with required courses where students just go in there and pass, especially in pass/fail courses. They just want to learn enough to get by. If you break your neck in a pass/fail course some people would say that's stupid. Why break your neck? Just get enough to pass the course. You have to get by that whole grade thing, and that's what I would like to emphasize. You do have to get good grades if you want to go certain places beyond college. I'm not so sure people look at your grade point averages in most businesses. They look at . . . "Do you get along with others? What are your human relations? How do . . ."

Al: Yeah! Let me break in. I have never run across an employer who asked for a grade point average, with the exception of the telephone company. The Telephone Company tends to hire managers according to GPA. But with more employers it is just the matter of . . . "What school did you go to? What was your major?" They don't ask what your GPA was. Myself, part of my problem when going to school, especially during the first three years, was that I did not realize that there was a difference between learning what interested you . . . that that was different than learning to pass the course with a good grade. Because I felt if I was learning something interesting and that I was growing as a person, then that would give me a good grade in the course. But it didn't work that way.

Tim: No.

Al: I kept getting average grades and somehow falling short. It took me a long time to realize I needed to do two kinds of learning: one was the learning just to satisfy my curiosity, and second was the kind of learning that it took to get a better grade in the course.

Tim: That is a crucial discrimination.

Al: My attitude was pretty much that when I got out in the real world on my own someplace and had a job, what was going to count was what kind of learning I had inside my head . . .

Tim: Exactly.

Al: . . . not how well I did in a course.

Tim: But very few students come to realize that. Most students are just interested in passing courses. I almost throw up every time I see students taking all kinds of pills and things like that to stay awake. When they are all through with the course and walk out in the hall, they say, "Boy, I hope I never see that book again. I am just so tired of this course." They seem to have this attitude of wanting to just get it over with. Why go to school if you just want to get it over with?

Al: I think that might be partly society's problem. The norm is that if you are a healthy person you graduate from high school and you to to college. Many students are not there for any inner feeling or any desire to learn very much at all. Some from curiosity, sure, but not a strong motivation to learn.

They're there because it was programmed into them. To me it's understandable why people feel that way.

Tim: There are just some really lousy courses that people have to take. I'll admit that there are some courses that people have to take that are boring, and poorly taught, and all of that. But you've got to take them, and the thing to do is to learn to take them to get the most reward and least pain out of them. It's like every job. Every job is going to gave its good days and its bad days. It has good parts and bad parts. There's little I hate more than a person who is going through his job during the day and he's yelling and screaming about . . . "This is such a painful task" . . . "I can't wait until the day is over." It just makes it a pain for everyone who works around him. It's really a pleasure to see people going through some hard work, which may not be the best part of the day for them, but they go through it cheerfully and make it not all that bad. They have learned to do it with a positive outlook. They say that "there is a reward at the end of this for me." I went through with friends a lot of courses we didn't want to take. They were very tough courses, and not that intellectually stimulating, but we had to take them. We did it with a lot of camaraderie. Because we did it together, we made sure that we all did well. I like the idea of studying in groups because sometimes the best time to get a group of people together is when you've got an especially tough course. You really need that stimulation from one another. You say, "Hey, you're going to make it. You're doing well." Math courses were always that way for me. I really needed extra stimulation from other people.

Al: You are right. This goes along with being a better student. I found that, especially my senior year. I made sure I always got into these last minute question-answer groups before the final exams.

Tim: Right.

Al: It gets so that after awhile, when you get used to taking tests and you start getting yourself organized, you start relaxing a little bit more. You know there is always going to be another test next week. They are just going to keep coming.

Tim: Right.

Al: So you just relax and you do the best you can at each one. The question-and-answer sessions really were extremely useful to me.

Tim: It sure takes care of your ulcers and colon, I'll tell you that. You don't get all hepped up and you don't get all nervous because you don't say, "Oh, gosh, what's gonna be on that test. I'm sort of worried about it. I just can't stand thinking about that test." Instead, you say, "I think I know what is going to be on that test and I'm not all that worried. This is what is going to have to be done. I'm gonna know this information. I'm going to take it and go on to the next one." Otherwise, college just becomes a day-by-day escape from something worse. Each day you are trying to escape from knowing that you are going to have to go on to something worse the next day. Test after test after test isn't a ball.

153

Al: When you were an undergraduate, did you expect to go to graduate school?

Tim: I thought I probably would, but I didn't know how I would pull it off after my first two years of college!

Al: Right!

Tim: Those were really trouble. I had very little confidence. Let me tell you a little story about how I picked up on a lot of the study skills stuff before I got it from working at the Reading Improvement Service. I had a friend whose name was Bill. He was in psychology and was a topnotch student. He was a Phi Beta Kappa when he was an undergraduate and he had gone on to Michigan's Ph.D. program in psychology. He was a guy who would come around my fraternity house all the time. You never saw this guy with a book during the night. He was always up in the fraternity going from room to room talking to the guys and getting guys to go to shows, and out having fun times. The rest of us were just breaking our necks. It was unbelievable. I said, "Bill, how do you do it? You're Phi Beta Kappa!" He said, "I just learned to study effectively." He was sort of one of these nonchalant guys. He didn't say he didn't study. He just said, "I learned how to study effectively." So I was over at his place one Friday night. I came over there to study because I couldn't study at the fraternity house on a Friday night. He had a set of rooms at his place and he was letting me use one. He was going out on a date, and I said, "Bill, do you have five minutes?" and he said "Sure." I said, "Tell me, how do you study?" He said, "What I do, Tim, is walk around the room and talk to myself as though I was talking to a professor and the other students about the answers to important questions. I talk to myself about what is going to be on tests. And then I go check my books and see how my answers are." So he says, "I spend most of the early part of the day, maybe from 11 a.m. to 3 p.m. during the day just going back and forth over questions and answers, talking to myself. I'll go spend time with other guys who I know who are in the same courses and I sit and I talk to them about these things." "Well, then," I said, "you do study a lot." He said, "I do study a lot. When I read books, I look for the questions and answers I think are important in my area of study and then I go talk to people at the labs and places like that. I go sit down with the professors and talk to them about these things. They always think I am an interesting fellow because I come and ask them important questions." Those weren't his exact words but in essence that was what he was saying. I thought, "If he can do that, I can do it, too." So I started practicing doing that. I started walking around the room, talking to myself and writing questions and answers. I modeled after a very, very effective student. And then I would start going out at night and having a good time and drinking with the guys and going to movies and having more dates. I was a very good student because I saw an effective model. Prior to that he took me aside and said, "Tim, you are paranoid. You always talk to me about how you think you will do well in this course if the instructor likes you or if he doesn't ask questions you hadn't predicted he would give you." He said, "You got this paranoid dilemma about whether you are gonna make it through college because of the grace of God. You are one of these great externalizers. You think all these external forces are controlling you." He said, "That's non-sense. What's controlling you, what *should* control you, is you. You should sit down and say, "What do I have to do to make it in this course," and you should practice doing that. You should forget about the personality of the instructor; you should forget whether the class is boring; you should forget about what sort of books they are using; forget about all that because you have no control over it." And I said, "Say, thanks a lot, Bill, that's really neat of you." It turned out he went on to get a Ph.D., I got a Ph.D., and now we are both in the same area. I think that is most amusing. But it was a funny thing. They used to come up to him at the fraternity house and say, "Bill, how do you do it?" He never told anybody but me. But that got him in trouble when he was in graduate school, and I will tell you why. You are supposed to play a game when you are a Ph.D. student. You are always sup-posed to be there playing up to the professors, I found, at least at the school I went to. You had to be there conning the professors, at least a lot of them in certain Ph.D. programs did that. They spent a lot of time making it look like they were working, even though they weren't doing anything. Whereas Bill never did that. He went off and did his work and also had fun. They didn't like the idea that he was having fun, so they gave him a lot of trouble. They said, "You are not doing a lot of things our graduate students are doing. We don't see you at the library every night, and we don't see you doing this and we don't see you doing that." He said, "Look, man, I have published more articles than other graduate students do; I get better grades. What is the gripe?" The point is that he wasn't playing the role they ex-pected of him. There is a part about humility in this type of thing. You have to learn to be humble.

AI: Or give the impression of working hard. I had a guy who wanted me to teach some public seminars that he was going to promote. He had a lot of ex-perience promoting and managing rock groups. He attended my seminars and when we were talking about how to improve my presentation, he said there is one thing I should do that he felt was necessary. He said, "You are smart; you know your stuff but you make it look too easy. The key to suc-cess of any rock group is that they work hard. If they show up and play their instruments and sing their songs and do it with a minimum amount of energy, people don't feel that they have gotten their money's worth." He said, "If you pay your $3 or $4 or $10 and they exhaust themselves on stage, screaming and yelling and moving and perspiring, you feel like you have gotten your money's worth." I've seen this principle in a number of different ways since he pointed it out to me. Many times people are skillful and they are accomplishing certain things, but it doesn't look like they are working very hard. The viewer tends to feel that if they are not working hard, they don't really deserve the rewards they are getting. It is the "work ethic" that is engrained in us to a certain extent. I was watching a television

155

show on circus performers and I suddenly realized when you watch one of these guys on the high wire there is usually some spot in their act where they start bouncing the wire back and forth as if they are almost going to fall off. This is just show business. Most of these high wire performers are so good they could walk across that wire relaxed, with no false movements and no close calls of any kind. But what they do is add that to the act because the audience feels that it is so dangerous. For their money they almost saw this guy get killed. Through good coordination and effort he survived that tough moment, and he made it through, and they give him a huge round of applause and believe he is one of the greatest they have ever seen . . . . because he added in that extra thing of almost falling. He is so good he really didn't have to do that.

Tim: That's right!

Al: I touched on this a little bit on one part of the book, suggesting to students, if they have a chance, that they look through lots of papers that students turn in and look for that element of hard work that shows through. If I get a paper that is half a page long and looks like it took about twenty minutes to write, that student is not going to get an A for that paper. The students who get As for the paper are the ones who have obviously put some time and effort into it. They asked questions; they did a little inquiry to find out what the answers were; they have gotten involved in this. There is an expenditure of energy that shows through in the papers that they have turned in. Usually I have to feel that before I feel comfortable at all in giving a student an A. It is not enough to jot down a few words.

Tim: You know, students learn that game quickly, sometimes to their detriment. I have a series of questions which I ask the students to answer after they read each of the 20 chapters in a book. I had a number of students who actually wrote down the questions; not only the answers but they wrote down the questions, too. It took twice as much writing. I said to them, "Why did you do that?" And they said, "I just wanted to show you that I was really interested." I replied, "You are just wasting hours of time doing that." I think it is that thing we were talking about before. Students sometimes think they are studying and doing well if they are putting in their time. If they are expending their energy and putting in their time they say, "Dammit, I am working and working hard and will get a good grade." And then when they get those lousy grades back, they say, "That no-good!"

Al: I worked hard.

Tim: I worked hard and I really got a rotten deal.

Al: Sure. I had something like that happen once when I was a Teaching Fellow. I started off the course and asked the students to do reading notes they were to turn in. This was the first set of reading notes, and most students' ranged from one to three pages. I had one student who turned in 150 pages of reading notes. Now, this is after the first two weeks of classes! There is no way she was going to cover five books and have done that much in the way of reading notes. So I rejected it, and I said, "This is much too much.

What's going on here?" As I talked to her, I found out she was a transfer student, and the impression I got was that she had a lot of her old term papers from her previous classes and she just put them together and handed them in. She was going to turn in so much that there would be no way I couldn't give her an A grade. But I didn't. I said, "I don't accept this, because this doesn't show what I wanted. It is more like a bunch of term papers." And her immediate reaction was . . . "You are out to get me. Why are you out to get me? Because this is O.K." In her mind, she had decided that this satisfied the requirement. She admitted the reading was done at her previous school, but she wouldn't listen to me when I said that book reports weren't the assignment. I started to get suspicious about her character. I took her paper and looked up the books she was supposedly citing and quoting and found out that these papers she turned in were highly plagiarized. I don't know what happened to get her out of the previous school, but it was obvious that there was something pretty phony going on. She got so wild about it, I had to turn it over to the Dean of Students. She was not only trying to con me with her 150 pages of reading notes, but what she turned in was not original. It was plagiarized. Yet she really believed that I hated her; I was out to get her; I was like all the other instructors at the other schools who had decided that she was not going to make it through college. Man, I really had a case on my hands.

Tim: Sometimes I don't fault a person like that because they don't really know. They never had somebody say to them, "Look, if you do this you are going to make it. Do these things; study effectively by doing these things. You won't have to do all that other garbage. It is like people you run into who like to make the super great impression the first time. Recently I ran into a guy who said, "I am Joe Dokes, a nice guy." I almost threw up. I have had several people do that to me. There is some big thing going around lately, about saying, "Sam Jones, a nice guy," or "A friendly fellow," or "A guy you would like to see more often." I think, "Why are you trying to make the big first impression on me?" It is superstitious and meaningless behavior which they think will get them somewhere.

Al: I have not had enough nerve to do it, but along the line of not being too friendly at first if you want friends, I have thought several times of walking up when I first meet somebody and say, "Hello, I am not going to say that I am pleased to meet you, because you will probably be as biased and narrow a human as most people."

Tim: And people won't buy the book if you say that! And that last story about that girl. If a student read that, she would say, "He's unfair. She did a lot of hard work, didn't she? She did 150 pages for Dr. Siebert and he flunked her." Some people would really be mad. But I agree with you; that happens in all schools. There are certain students we all know are con artists. They come and they try to spend most of their time with you talking, just spending time with you and trying to convince you what nice guys they are. I am tempted to say, "Look, man, it's not that I don't like you, but I got

	350 other students." They figure the way to get a grade is to be your friend.
Al:	That is their approach. Unfortunately, with a few professors, it works.
Tim:	It really does. I've seen instructors spend hours of their time with one or two students and give the students higher grades than they've earned.
Al:	Did you ever play up to profs?
Tim:	Never. I avoided talking to them . . . until my senior year when I started asking questions I wanted answers to.
Al:	I wouldn't talk to profs. I'd get nervous. It wasn't until graduate school that I called a prof by his first name, and that was because he ordered me to. In my case, becoming a better student, I see a series of things that happened. One was self-image. Once I became aware of this, then I could look back at a specific example of how self-image made me get low grades my first two years. I went to college when a number of the kids I ran around with in high school went to the same college. There was this one guy I really looked up to. He was a "big man on campus." He was very mature, could date almost any girl that he chose to be interested in.
Tim:	Suave . . . .
Al:	He was so suave. He could talk on a friendly basis to professors and not be embarrassed like me or nervous. We were taking a freshman chemistry course. He was pre-med and I was pre-med. I listened to the professor and I read the first chapter in my chemistry book. The professor announced he would have a weekly quiz each Friday. So I took the first weekly quiz and I got 100%. My idol, the intelligent, sophisticated, suave, capable, mature person got 85%. It shocked me that he got 85% and I got 100%. So the next week we took the weekly quiz again. That time I didn't read my chemistry book as much. He got 89% or something close and I got 90%. I *still* beat him! It took me about three or four weeks before I was able to consistently get a score of 70% on the weekly quizzes, which seemed to me to be appropriate, considering that this guy's level was about 85–90%. And considering my relationship to him, it did seem reasonable. I am not saying there was a lot of conscious thought going on, but looking back, I can see that each time I got a better grade than he did, I stopped studying so hard. I stopped preparing for the test; I stopped taking such good notes in the class. I just started acting in ways that led to my getting a grade that fit my self-image as measured against him.
Tim:	I used to see that with a lot of guys, with the athletes around school. If you went to class, you had your jacket on and just sat there and listened and chatted with the girls and things like that; made coffee dates; took a few notes. At the end, you would try to get some old tests or things like that and try to make it through. There is that image that some guys live up to. It seems that one of the key things to getting good grades is to not have a loser's image. It's to say to yourself and say, "I'm not too personally concerned with how I look to this professor, or how I look to others. I am concerned about how I look to myself. What do I really want to be able to do here, independent of what others think of me?" Then you set those goals

up for yourself. You say, "I want to get good grades here. And I'll spend so much time doing that. Now, if my friends happen to go along with this, that's great; if they don't, maybe I need new friends."

Al: To me that's a second or third step. The first step, it seems to me, is just to spend a little time fantasizing about what would it be like if I got a good grade and you go through, mentally, all the important people; the person you are dating, your roommate, people in the dorm, friends you graduated from high school with, parents, teachers back at high school. And just think, what if I got an A in this course and so on and so forth. What if my mother found out; my sister found out; if my date found out I was getting As. A lot of kids can't handle that. They *cannot* handle it if someone found out they were getting As, because it just doesn't fit with what other people perceive them as. And so they act in ways consistent with other people's perceptions that they are very mediocre.

Tim: That's true. When you find yourself acting in ways which are different from those people's perceptions of what you should be, sometimes you catch a lot of flack for it. But if students act in those ways and change their performance, they become better students, and a lot of their old friends fall by the wayside. Not that this is a bad thing either. It is just that their interests change, they go into different things, and their friends' interests change and they go into different things. Naturally that happens as a person changes throughout life. You often feel bad about this and you say, "Hey, I don't see so and so anymore." But when you think about it, it may be because you are a new and different person. Your interests and your goals may be totally different from those of your old friends. Then you go back to the tenth year or twentieth year high school reunion and you say, "Isn't this strange?"

Al: Relating to what I was saying about acting in ways consistent with what other people expect, this is exactly what women have been struggling with for a long time. And many women, to be "nice" people, kept themselves fairly weak, subservient in a way that would not threaten the male ego or the male status because the man could not handle it. It's like saying, "I love you, and because I love you, I will help you avoid experiencing distress or nervousness. If I were to be strong, you would feel that way; so to keep you from being upset, I will keep myself weak." And there are a lot of people who make that choice.

Tim: I think what we are saying to the student is, "Look, you've got a choice."

Al: Most people don't realize it is a choice.

Tim: I said that to myself when I was going to drop out of college. I said, "You've got a choice. You can either go back there, and gut it out and figure out how to do it more efficiently and effectively, or you can quit. But if you quit, what is going to happen to you?" So you go back and you find out— There are some very, very simple ways of improving the means by which you get through school. And once you do that, you have a lot more fun in life. I am not saying there is any great sort of extraspecial experience. It

159

is just a matter of: You do this and this is what happens. You can't beat that.

Al: What does our book accomplish that other books don't?

Tim: I think it compiles and condenses the most effective set of study techniques from various learning and study skill centers. In preparing the book, I spent a considerable amount of time just looking over what everybody else had done. And I concluded several things. One, almost every book was far too large and asked people to do things which, in fact, were really very questionable procedures. In essence, we are suggesting those things which are most effective in helping students become more successful. I didn't include anything that I didn't use with a large number of students and which wasn't recommended by a lot of other well-known people in the field.

Al: We certainly have an unusual combination here, with your strong emphasis on the behavioral approach and my focus of attention toward introspection, self-examination, visualization, self-image, self-development, and such. I'm pleasantly amazed at how well our approaches have meshed. I think I know why, though; because I use descriptive rather than hypothetical constructs.

Tim: Whatever you did, yours is the first description of self-actualization that has made sense to me. Everything else I've read is unintelligible.

A.:   We certainly have an interesting combination. One thing I would say is that we have written a book that I wish I had had when I was first starting college.

Tim: Many students who have talked to me about prepublication copies of things that are in this book have said things such as, "That's really good. I wish I could have had that when I was a freshman in high school or a freshman in college. Can I have a copy of this?" or "Can I Xerox a copy of this to give to my brother who is starting college?"—or to my nephew or my son. They really like it because it is in layman's terms. Things are easy to understand; not a lot of psychological mumbo jumbo which they couldn't go out and apply.

Al: And having put together a lot of practical tips, we don't say that they have to do it. It's, "Here is what you might find will work for you if you choose to be a better student, and these are things that other students and we have been able to make work. Give it a shot and see if it works for you."

Tim: Every one of the things that I have suggested in this book I have used with large numbers of students. I started using these techniques in 1968. I have had all types of students with a variety of problems. One of the things I really think is interesting about what we have done is the fact that, when I ran into these students, a large number of them were having psychological problems, *supposedly*. They were having self-image problems, self-esteem problems, low ego, however psychologists want to classify them. The main thing that makes students feel better is doing better in their classes. It's like psychologists want to give everybody therapy, give them special counseling, give them special this, give them special that, and they overlook the key problem. That is, you can't feel good about yourself in school and college unless you can do well in class. It sure helps your self-esteem if you can go to class and answer questions and ask good questions and feel good about yourself in the majority of your working day. I don't care how much money you pay most people, they are not going to stay in jobs long unless they like what they are doing. I believe that from personal experience. Students will come to me and say, "Everything is terrible," and I say, "How are your grades going? How is school going?" And the student says, "That's the main problem. So I say, "Let's focus on that." And then they say, "But . . . I am having a problem with my girl . . . my parents are doing this . . . " I say, "I am a study skills counselor. I am going to help you get better grades; help you read better; help you do all these things students should do better. Let's work on one thing at a time. If you feel you've got problems in other areas, go to the counseling center." That's one of the problems I see in colleges, especially in counseling centers. They are trying to help students solve academic problems by working on social problems. Very few schools have real true academic improvement centers. Or they may have a small reading improvement program, but seldom do you get somebody who can help you learn to write better and to study better and all of those things.

Al: In the Student Counseling Center, oftentimes you get a psychologist . . .

Tim: Maybe a social worker.

Al: . . . or other persons there. They are the counselor types, and they accept the definition of the problem because it is what they were trained to do. Because a kid keeps having a problem with girls or boys or whatever. So they figure if they can get this personality shaped up, maybe the grades will improve.

Tim: But the students still don't know how to study. We used to have graduate students come in and say, "My parents spent all this money, I spent all this money, I work all the time, and I am not making it through school." We'd test them and they'd have a sixth or seventh or eighth grade reading level. Then, they'd probably have medical textbooks that they read and reread. You can't do that, keep rereading a medical textbook. Students are doing what I consider punishing and injurious psychological behaviors. They are involved in a behavior which has no payoff towards the goal they are trying to accomplish. It is a really very painful thing. They waste hundreds of hours.

Al: There is lots of wasted time.

Tim: The best example I can think of—I remember doing this in my sophomore year. I was taking an American History course and everybody said, "Outline your books, use the yellow markers." I took a history book which was 700 and something pages. I outlined half of the entire book in preparation for the test. A big, gigantic history book. And halfway through I said to myself, "Are you crazy? What are you going to do with these outlines once you are done?" If you pick up a book on study skills, a lot of them say practice outlining the book. They suggest a lot of crazy things that, in fact, don't work. And I finally said, "Ugh! I'll never outline another book in my life." And I never did.

Al: So this is why, in our whole thing on student success, there has not once been any mention of taking a yellow marker or a ruler and underlining or highlighting the important words and phrases.

Tim: No! What do you have when it is all over? You've got a bunch of books that are underlined. How are you going to study? Go through the book and look at the important underlined things? . . . It can be all right if you want to underline and circle answers to questions. I know people who do that. They say, "Here is an answer to a question." And I say, "Yes, the question was this and here is the answer." And they see they know the answer. That is one thing. Going through and circling or marking what you know are important answers to questions. But just to underline and underline every time you see another important point or outline notes because that is what you practice in school! Remember making outlines?

Al: Right. Some students use underlinings to try to help pay attention to what they are reading. The only time I use a yellow marker is when I find a statement the author makes that I think I might come back and quote some day, or I want to be able to find the statement quickly, I'll use a yellow marker down the border or maybe to highlight some phrases in sentences, but I will only do this maybe two or three times in an entire book.

Tim: You have to make yourself ask whenever you do something like this, "How is this going to help me to do better on a test?" or "help me ask or answer an important question?" Many people suggest things to students, which if they ever did themselves, they would find out they were burdens and a waste of time. They're good things to do if you plan to spend twelve hours a day studying. You enjoy reading and rereading and going over outlines and underlining pages, etc., etc. I am not saying you can't pick up the information that way, but it is very tough to put it all together. What happens is that you're very good at memorizing large bodies of information.

Al: Either that or you just practice recognition.

Tim: Right, and what's that good for? The best example I can give of how I realized how useless all that was was when I went home and got out two gigantic boxes of all the notes I took during my first two to three years of college. I browsed through them and I didn't recognize a thing. Why? Because all I did was practice outlining, remembering, and recognizing stuff. And, interestingly enough, after looking at my graduate notes, all those notes are familiar. They were all very important. They covered topics which I got to know very well. I am sure that is true with most people. You take your college notes and you could throw them out the door and never see them again and you haven't lost anything. People say, "Well, if you were forced to, you could remember that stuff and it would make it very meaningful." No, it wouldn't. It's meaningless information. I no more could tell you about the anthropology of American Indians or the geography of

Australia than I could the day I entered the course. And I think that is tragic. An education is something you should be able to take with you.

Al: Well, you've got to acknowledge there is going to be a lot of forgetting that takes place no matter *what* approach you use.

Tim: Yes, but when I am to the point where I don't even know where Australia is on the map . . .

Al: (laughing) Come on, Tim!

Tim: . . . I couldn't tell you where the Navajo lived! . . . The point I am trying to get across to the students is, "Don't waste your time." Figure out where you want to go, how you're going to get there, and how you know you've arrived. At the end of the day, if you can't say, "I've accomplished this, this, and this and I have studied this, this, and this, and now I can do better in this course because I know this and I didn't know it when I started out the day," then you are wasting your time.

Al: I have to disagree with you on that, because I believe that it's an equally okay, valid, legitimate way to go through life, getting up each morning and following your curiosity. I'm not saying every morning, but some mornings. Tim, you just made a pretty tight statement, like at the end of *each* day say I accomplished this, this, and this.

Tim: Something good has happened. I can do this that I couldn't do before.

Al: I think people are better off if they have some more throwaway time, where they don't accomplish anything. In fact, the purpose of it is to not accomplish something. To have a day where you are not working or accomplishing anything.

Tim: But what you might accomplish is just the fact that you relax and do nothing and you know that is good for you. Some people can't even say at the end of the day, "I just sat and did nothing and it was good."

Al: For the person who does not do that *every* day.

Tim: For the person who does that every day, I think there may be some problems.

Al: Which gets us to what everyone of us runs into. That is, no matter what we are doing, there is going to be someone who comes along and is unhappy about it. If a person is very relaxed and casual and doesn't accomplish a whole lot, someone says, "Hey, you ought to accomplish more." With a person who is accomplishing an awful lot, someone says, "Hey, slow down. You ought to relax and not try to accomplish so much." There will always be someone wanting people to be different from however they are.

Tim: In essence, we are saying to students to be whatever they want to be. And if they want to be better students, here are some things that they can do to help them get there. It's their choice. If they want to, fine; if they don't want to, they can sell the book back.

Al: No, they can't! How about saying they should sell their book to someone else!

Tim: I'll buy that!

ACKNOWLEDGEMENTS

This book is the result of the contributions of many people . . .

The many unnamed educators whose striving for improvement made available the large body of knowledge that we drew from.

Professor James V. McConnell, who advised each of us during our respective graduate years and then arranged for the meshing of talents of two people from different perspectives and opposite shores.

Professor Wilbert J. McKeachie, whose many years of dedicated effort to improve teaching and whose personal support of beginning instructors created an exciting growth atmosphere at the University of Michigan.

The Holt publishers who saw the need for the book and contributed to its development, with special thanks to Ray Ashton, Dan Loch, Jeanette Johnson, and Marjorie Marks.

The many students who used the early versions and gave us helpful feedback.

The manuscript readers who gave us valuable suggestions.

Our supportive friends and companions, who gave us sustained encouragement and many useful suggestions.

Our animal friends, whose involvement in the work on our desks kept us aware of how important it is to have time for friends.

Al and Tim

FEEDBACK REQUEST

Do you have any study tips, comments, constructive criticism, or suggestions you would like to pass along to us? If so, please send them to us c/o:

Psychology Editor
College Department
Holt, Rinehart & Winston
383 Madison Avenue
New York, NY 10017

What did you find of most value in this book?

In what ways might it be improved?

Other comments: